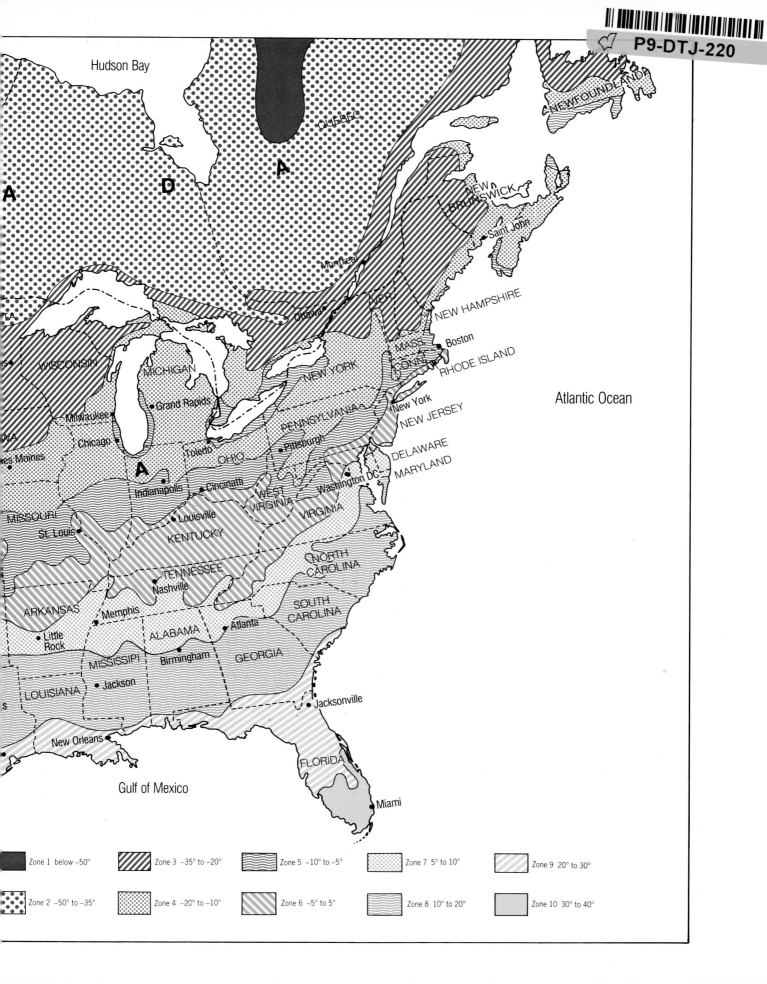

P9-DTJ-220

Hudson Bay

QUEBEC

A

D

A

Montreal

Ottawa

NEWFOUNDLAND

NEW BRUNSWICK

Saint John

NEW HAMPSHIRE

Boston

MASS

CONN

RHODE ISLAND

Atlantic Ocean

WISCONSIN

MICHIGAN

NEW YORK

Grand Rapids

Milwaukee

PENNSYLVANIA

New York

NEW JERSEY

Chicago

Toledo

Pittsburgh

DELAWARE

es Moines

OHIO

Washington DC

MARYLAND

A

Indianapolis

Cincinatti

WEST VIRGINIA

MISSOURI

Louisville

VIRGINIA

St. Louis

KENTUCKY

NORTH CAROLINA

TENNESSEE

Nashville

ARKANSAS

Memphis

SOUTH CAROLINA

ALABAMA

Atlanta

Little Rock

MISSISSIPPI

Birmingham

GEORGIA

Jackson

LOUISIANA

Jacksonville

New Orleans

FLORIDA

Gulf of Mexico

Miami

Zone 1 below −50°

Zone 3 −35° to −20°

Zone 5 −10° to −5°

Zone 7 5° to 10°

Zone 9 20° to 30°

Zone 2 −50° to −35°

Zone 4 −20° to −10°

Zone 6 −5° to 5°

Zone 8 10° to 20°

Zone 10 30° to 40°

Fuchsias

Hardiness Zones

The hardiness-zone system illustrated on the end flaps divides northern North America into ten zones based upon average minimum temperatures. The bands run generally in an east-west direction and range from the treeless area in the extreme north of Canada (Zone 1), where temperatures may fall to − 50 degrees F, to the southernmost tip of Florida (Zone 10), where minimum temperatures may be as high as 40 degrees F.

In the United States, fuchsias' flowering season will vary according to the zone in which the plant is grown; this season occurs later in the colder zones, earlier in the warmer zones. Individual fuchsias illustrated in this book have not been assigned specific hardiness-zone ratings because most fuchsias are not ''hardy'' plants – they will not survive frost.

FUCHSIAS

JILL R. CLARK

PHOTOGRAPHS BY DAVID CLARK

The Globe Pequot Press

Chester, Connecticut

First American edition published in 1988 by
The Globe Pequot Press, Chester, Connecticut 06412

Library of Congress Cataloging-in-Publication Data

Clark, Jill R.
Fuchsias.

(Classic garden plants)
Bibliography: p.
Includes index.
1. Fuchsia.   I. Title.   II. Series.
SB413.F8C59   1988   635.9′3344   88–9520
ISBN O–87106–709–9

Produced by the Justin Knowles Publishing Group,
9 Colleton Crescent, Exeter, Devon, England

Photographs: David Clark
Illustrations: Vana Haggerty

Zone map reproduced by courtesy of Swallow Books Ltd

Manufactured in Portugal

CONTENTS

LIST OF PLATES

FOREWORD

In recent years fuchsia growers around the world have learned more about their fellow enthusiasts and the plants they grow through personal visits and correspondence, the exchange of journals between societies, and the distribution of excellent books such as this. One result has been an increase in the number of fuchsia cultivars registered voluntarily with the American Fuchsia Society's International Registrar – 215 in 1987 alone. This increase in registration, along with the publication of detailed cultivar descriptions in the annual Fuchsia Registry, has called attention to the large number of newly bred fuchsias offered to the public each year. In this book Jill Clark describes and displays a wide choice of beautiful fuchsias both old and new, enough to decorate a large garden with a rich variety of forms and colors.

Why, then, should hybridizers need to produce still more cultivars – except, of course, to satisfy our impulse to try something new? Without a doubt most of us feel comfortable with familiar forms, and new plants that are radically different are likely to be rejected. Yet some argue that there are too many look-alike fuchsias and that new ones look *too* familiar, a result of most modern fuchsias being derived from only a few of the original species.

With the goal of adding 'new blood' to cultivated fuchsias, members of the Hybridizing Committee of the Netherlands Circle of Fuchsia Friends are doing some pioneering work in fuchsia breeding. They have been using species collected and distributed over the past few years by American taxonomists P. Berry and D. Breedlove under the direction of Peter Raven of the Missouri Botanical Garden. New flower forms and uncommon colors – like eggplant purple, derived from the New Zealand species – will surely be produced in increasing numbers by the Dutch and other hybridizers.

For many years we have classified two groups of fuchsias by parentage: the orange-red, heat-tolerant hybrids of *F. triphylla* (such as 'Gartenmeister Bonstedt') and the frost-resistant, miniature-flowered hybrids of Section *encliandra* (such as 'Chance Encounter'). With the introduction of new genetic material into fuchsia hybridizing, future generations can expect to see additional interesting classifications based on parentage. Different yet uncommonly beautiful cultivars will add zest to our fuchsia-growing experiences.

For the time being, however, fuchsias in cultivation are still classified principally by growth habit and flower form. Flower color is of primary importance to buyers, and fuchsias offer many pleasing choices, as David Clark's photographs show so strikingly in this book. Integrity of habit, form, and color is important, especially to exhibitors. We want trailing varieties whose branches arch gracefully downward, bush varieties that stand strongly erect, and still others that bend willingly into many decorative forms. Flowers should be plentiful, have good substance, and hold their colors well. Gardeners who grow fuchsias in harsher climates want varieties offering an extra measure of frost resistance or heat tolerance. Jill Clark skillfully guides us through all the pleasant aspects of fuchsia gardening, from choosing beautiful specimens to growing them in ways that satisfy both their cultural needs and our aesthetic preferences.

We have come to expect excellence from Jill and David Clark, authors of the popular *The Oakleigh Guide to Fuchsias* and winners of numerous gold medals for displays of fuchsias at the Chelsea Flower Show in London. They have not disappointed us; this is a delightful, well-written, and beautifully illustrated fuchsia book.

Chuck Hassett
Editor, American Fuchsia Society Bulletin

INTRODUCTION

In the spring, many people are tempted to buy fuchsias from nurseries and garden centres as summer bedding plants. Quite often the plants perform so well and give so much pleasure that a fuchsia enthusiast is born.

This book was written to help the fuchsia grower through the early stages of propagation and cultivation and on to the production of better plants for garden decoration or prize-winning specimens for exhibition. Gardening is a subtle blend of art and science and eventually all growers develop their own individual skills. Much of the pleasure lies in developing these techniques and in choosing cultivars that particularly appeal from the many thousands available.

The colour illustrations and descriptive text cover about two hundred fuchsias that are easily obtainable in the United States and Europe; they are also representative of most of the cultivars grown today. The colour of the fuchsia flower and even the habit of the plant can, though, vary considerably depending on the cultural conditions under which the plant is grown.

The sections on cultivation (pages 16–21) and on overwintering non-hardy fuchsias (pages 121–2) apply to those countries that experience winters in which the temperature drops below freezing for considerable periods. For fuchsia growers in those countries who do not possess a heated greenhouse, other ways are described for successfully overwintering plants. Fuchsias are also grown in warm countries where frost is not a problem, but the flowers may need protection from dryness and a hot sun. In a mild climate fuchsias are not rested in the winter months but grow and flower year round.

Many of the newer fuchsias now reaching Europe from the United States, New Zealand, and Australia are very large-flowered, flamboyant cultivars that are increasingly popular with the general public. The serious exhibitor, while growing these for their novelty value, will also continue to grow those cultivars that have been tried and tested over the years. Indeed, many of the most popular fuchsias available today were also great favourites with the Victorians.

The fuchsia has been immensely popular in the past and is again at a peak of popularity; we may hope that future generations will come to admire, grow, and perpetuate a genus of singularly attractive flowering plants.

THE HISTORY OF FUCHSIAS

Fuchsias make up a large distinctive genus of about one hundred species that grow in the Andes, from Colombia and Venezuela in the north to Tierra del Fuego in the south, in Hispaniola, and in the mountains of Brazil, Mexico, and Central America. There is also a small disparate section in New Zealand and Tahiti. The earliest fossil of fuchsia pollen, found in New Zealand, was laid down about thirty million years ago, but, because there are so many fuchsia species, it is generally accepted that the genus probably evolved considerably earlier, in South America.

The fuchsia plants we grow today certainly had their origins in Central and South America, and the earliest man-made recordings of fuchsias are carvings made about a thousand years ago on rock faces and in caves by early tribes of South American Indians. It was not until the 17th century, however, that the colonization of America opened up the continent to the Western World. Living there was hard and fraught with danger and disease; many plants were an indispensable part of everyday life and were used for medicines, flavourings, insect repellants, dyes, tonics, cosmetics, and for smoking. Plants were of such importance at this time that it was a great era for botanists, naturalists, and plant collectors. One such botanist was Father Charles Plumier, a missionary, who, during his travels in the West Indies, discovered many new plants that he recorded and drew. Between 1689 and 1697, during a stay in Haiti, he found a new genus of plant. He was in the habit of naming new plants after famous naturalists, and he named his new discovery after Leonhard Fuchs, an eminent professor of medicine who was born in 1501 and died in 1566. A great plant lover, Fuchs published in 1542 a herbal, *De Historia Stirpium*, and in its preface wrote:

> ... there is no reason why I should dilate at greater length upon the pleasantness and delights of acquiring knowledge of plants, since there is no one who does not know that there is nothing in this life pleasanter and more delightful than to wander over woods, mountains, plains ... and to gaze intently on them. But it increases that pleasure and delight not a little if there be an acquaintance with the virtues and powers of these same plants.

Like us, he would certainly have felt 'pleasure and delight' in being acquainted with the virtues of the beautiful genus that bears his name.

Father Plumier published his findings in 1703 in his book *Nova Plantarum Americanarum Genera*. He called the new plant *Fuchsia triphylla flore coccinea* and, although the illustrations of it in his book are poor, it is undoubtedly what is today called *Fuchsia triphylla*. (The shortened name was given to it by Linnaeus in the first edition of his *Species Plantarum*.) No plants found their way to Europe at this time, and no more specimens of *F. triphylla* were discovered for some hundred and seventy years – by which time people were beginning to doubt its existence. However, in 1872 an American, Thomas Hogg, sent from the West Indies to Europe seed collected in the vicinity of Santo Domingo that proved to be that of *F. triphylla*.

Meanwhile, though, other species of fuchsia had been discovered and sent to Europe. The first species to arrive in England was *F. coccinea*, a native of Brazil, which was donated to Kew Gardens by a Captain Firth in 1788. In the same year, the same fuchsia species was acquired by an English nurseryman, James Lee, who saw the potential of the plant and by 1793 had propagated sufficient stocks for general sale. The fuchsia proved a very popular plant and other nurseries eagerly sponsored expeditions to find more species. During the first half of the 19th century many more were found and put on sale, including *F. lycioides*, *F. magellanica*, *F. arborescens*, and *F. fulgens*. The first attempts at hybridization were made early in the 19th century, but no significant cultivars were recorded until 1840. At this time a chance seedling was raised by a gardener to a clergyman living in southern England. This cultivar was distributed under the name of 'Venus Victrix' and was remarkable for being the first cultivar with a white tube and sepals and a purple corolla. This new colour combination made it a desirable parent plant for further crosses, and it was extensively used for the production of other superior cultivars. In 1850 the first double fuchsia flower was produced by a Mr Story, a nurseryman from Newton Abbot in the west of England, who went on to produce many other cultivars, the most famous of which was 'Queen Victoria', which had a double flower with red sepals and a white corolla. Story also released the first fuchsia with a striped corolla; it has not, however, survived in cultivation.

There were hybridists at work in most other European countries, notably France, Belgium, and Germany. The nursery of Lemoine in France introduced over four hundred new cultivars many of which – including 'Monsieur Thibaut' (see pages 97–9), 'Molesworth' (see page 67), 'Phenomenal', and 'Abbé Farges' (see page 83) – are still in general cultivation. Another notable cultivar produced in France, by a raiser called Crousse in 1861, was 'Bon Accorde' (see page 77), which was the first plant to have upward-looking flowers. A Belgian grower, Cornelissen, was known particularly for his red and white cultivars, the most

The parts of a fuchsia.
1 Leaf node.   2 Ovary.
3 Tube.   4 Sepals.
5 Corolla (petals).
6 Stigma.   7 Stamens.
Fuchsia flowers are classified in
three groups: single, semi-
double, and double. A single
flower has only four petals, a
semi-double has between five and
eight petals, and flowers with
more than eight petals are
regarded as double.

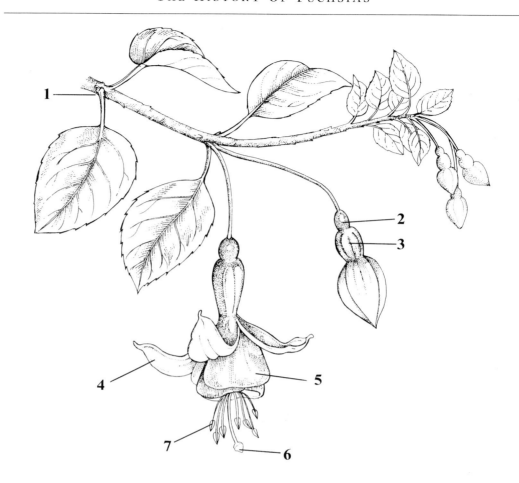

famous of which is 'Madame Cornelissen' a very free-flowering, hardy fuchsia. From the German nurserymen Rehnelt and Bonstedt came the beautiful Triphylla hybrids which resulted from crosses using Plumier's *F. triphylla* as one of the parent plants. 'Gartenmeister Bonstedt' (see page 93) is a good example, although, in common with all other Triphylla cultivars, it is rather tender and requires a minimum winter temperature of at least 45°F (7.5°C).

Fuchsias reached their peak of popularity in Britain in the second half of the 19th century. The Victorians loved plants and the wealthy built large conservatories to grow the more tender ones. Wages were very low and many gardeners were employed on the large estates; they could spend hours training fuchsia plants into fantastic shapes for exhibition and for the decoration of garden parties and other social functions. One such gardener was James Lye, who exhibited such well-grown plants that he was described in 1886 as the champion fuchsia grower in the west of England. He was also a prolific hybridizer; his cultivars are still noted for their creamy white tubes and sepals. One of his best is 'Lye's Unique', a single flower with waxy white tube and sepals and a soft orange corolla, raised in

13

1886. James Lye's daughter married another grower and exhibitor of fuchsias, George Bright, who produced some good cultivars of his own, including 'Coachman' (see page 62). During the early 1900s, Bright was showing pillars and pyramids of even better quality than his father-in-law's.

The Victorians also used fuchsias as cut flowers, the graceful arching sprays being well suited to the multi-tiered floral containers and epergnes so popular at the time. The fuchsia's popularity began to decline with the outbreak of World War I. Growing space was needed for edible crops and the young men who had tended the gardens and plants went off to the war from which many never returned. The large estates began to be broken up, and the survivors could no longer afford to employ numbers of gardeners.

The gradual revival of interest in fuchsias after the war was initiated in California, with the formation in 1929 of the American Fuchsia Society. Members of the society travelled to Europe to select cultivars that would flourish in California and could be used also as parent plants. This resulted in a wave of new hybridizing that produced many new and varied flower forms and colours. H. M. Tiret of San Francisco produced many popular cultivars, including 'Swingtime' (see page 137), 'Leonora' (see page 131), and 'Jack Shahan' (see page 130). Victor Reiter raised 'Flying Cloud' (see page 129), 'Red Spider', 'Trail Blazer' (see pages 137–8), and 'Mantilla' (see page 132). Hazard and Hazard in Pacific Grove, California, were also great hybridists. Their first introduction was 'Hap Hazard' and they went on to produce nearly seventy more, including 'Flash' (see page 128) and 'Chang'. Their 1930 catalogue described seventy-six cultivars and was the most complete list of its day. Gus Neiderholzer of San Francisco was responsible for over one hundred and thirty new raisings, including 'Symphony' in 1944 and 'Collingwood' (see page 61) in 1945.

The production of new cultivars continued apace in the United States. One outstanding hybridist, Edward Paskesen, who died in 1979, raised the very beautiful cultivar 'Bicentennial' (see page 94), the first double flower that was predominantly orange. Annabelle Stubbs is now one of the leading hybridists in the USA, with over fifty exquisite introductions. Her most popular cultivars include 'Pink Marshmallow' (see page 134), 'Applause' (see page 123), 'Dancing Flame' (see page 128), and 'Nancy Lou' (see page 76).

The American Fuchsia Society was in 1967 appointed the International Authority for Fuchsia Registration and Nomenclature by the International Society for Horticultural Science. Every cultivar registered with the American Fuchsia Society is allocated an official number and the name is checked to avoid duplication and subsequent confusion.

The British Fuchsia Society was founded in 1938 and managed to publish a year book to sustain the interest of its members throughout the difficult years of World War II. In the post-war years many of the society's members became hybridists, among them W. P. Wood, a retired gardener. His main interest was producing new hardy cultivars that could be grown permanently in the shrub border. His introductions include 'Joan Cooper' and 'Eleanor Rawlins', both accepted by the British Fuchsia Society as showbench hardies. Another keen member of the British Fuchsia Society for nearly thirty years was Cliff Gadsby, who died in 1978. He raised over eighty new cultivars and was particularly interested in those plants that carried their flowers erect. In 1964 he raised 'Upward Look', a cross of 'Athela' with 'Bon Accorde', and the first plant since 'Bon Accorde' itself to have its flowers held upwards. He produced many other outstanding fuchsias, including the exceptionally free-flowering 'Lady Isobel Barnett' (see page 91) and the hardy 'Prosperity', with its large, double, red and white flowers (see page 33). Other late-20th-century British hybridizers include Ron Holmes, Dr M. Ryle, Alfred Thornley, Wilfred Tolley, and Mrs E. Holmes, who raised the lovely 'Countess of Maritza' and 'Igloo Maid'.

The raising of new cultivars continues around the world, with recent introductions in Australia and New Zealand as well as the United States and Europe. One of the main problems for the future seems to be the vast number of similar cultivars now being introduced. There is always pressure on commercial nurserymen to introduce novelties each year, and this is leading to a flood of cultivars that show little, if any, improvement over existing cultivars.

CULTIVATION AND PROPAGATION

Growing conditions in the greenhouse

The fuchsia is a native plant of the sub-tropical regions, and it will not tolerate hot, dry conditions in summer or very cold, damp conditions in winter. On hot summer days, it is essential to provide maximum ventilation and to damp down the greenhouse floor. As the water gradually evaporates it will increase the atmospheric humidity. Evaporation causes cooling, so damping down also helps to reduce the temperature of the greenhouse. On very hot days, if the greenhouse is to be left without attention, old newspapers can be soaked with water and left on the pathway. Although fuchsias require good light levels for strong, sturdy growth, it is necessary to shade them during hot summer months to reduce the temperature inside the greenhouse; the smaller the house, the greater the shading that will be required. Blinds and netting are extremely effective and they can be removed easily in bad weather, when shading is not needed. The white- or green-coloured coating that may be painted on to the outside of the glass is another good and cheap method of shading. Sheets of newspaper may also be pinned up to provide temporary shading in small areas of the greenhouse.

The levels of temperature and humidity maintained in the greenhouse are important for healthy, disease-resistant growth. In the autumn and winter months, when the temperature falls and the air is damp, botrytis can become a problem and every effort should be made to provide maximum ventilation. Most cultivars grown in the greenhouse will need only minimal frost protection and can be overwintered at a temperature of 41°F (5°C). The type of heater used is not important as long as it can maintain this minimum temperature even on the coldest nights. Electric heating has the advantage of being a dry source of warmth, whereas oil produces water on burning, increasing atmospheric humidity and consequently the risk of botrytis.

Composts and potting

A choice must first be made between growing in clay or plastic pots. Clay pots are more porous and in the early critical stages plants growing in them are less likely to be overwatered. Evaporation of water from the pot surface also has the beneficial effect of cooling the plant roots. On the debit side, large well-established plants dry out much more quickly and constant watering can become a chore. Plastic pots are now more easily obtainable and cheaper to buy and they are lighter than clay pots, which can be an advantage. However, the extra weight of a clay pot can give increased stability to a tall standard fuchsia or other large plant. Plastic pots are easily cleaned and sterilized for re-use, and most modern potting composts are especially prepared for use in them. Plants grown in plastic pots do not need watering so frequently, but conversely it is very much easier to overwater young plants or freshly potted-on plants because the compost will take much longer to dry out. Black plastic pots can also create problems because black objects absorb rather than reflect heat, especially in direct sunlight, and consequently the plant roots may become overheated and die. The final choice of pot will ultimately depend on individual growing conditions and personal preference.

The next decision is which type of compost to use. Basically there are two types of potting composts – those that contain sterilized loam or soil and soilless mixtures containing peat or pulverized bark, sometimes mixed with grit or perlite. The most widely available soil-based compost is a mixture of partially sterilized loam together with peat, sand, chalk, and a base fertilizer. Soilless composts usually consist of a mixture of peat or pulverized bark with sharp sand, grit or perlite and a suitable fertilizer; chalk is added to adjust the acidity of the mixture.

Soil-based compost must be used within six weeks of mixing, otherwise chemical changes will alter its composition and cause plants potted in it to fail. Although soilless composts will also deteriorate with age and are best used fresh, they may be safely used for up to a year if stored under suitable conditions.

Cuttings that have been rooted in a loamless compost or peat block often show a marked reluctance to transfer to a soil-based type. However, bigger, more vigorous plants growing in 4in (10cm) or larger pots can be moved easily into soil-based compost without a check to growth. Cuttings rooted in a suitable soil-based compost can be transplanted into any other medium without problems.

High concentrations of plant nutrients can prove toxic and the great advantage of a soil-based compost is that it can hold safely a large quantity of the nutrients and slowly release them to the plant as required – it has what is known as a buffering effect. Nonetheless, be careful to avoid using too strong a grade – that is, one too rich in fertilizer – or the plant's roots will be scorched.

Good quality loam is difficult to obtain and soil-based composts can be very variable in quality. Soilless composts are accordingly now more widely used because ingredients of suitable quality are easily obtained and the use of standard constituents produces more uniform growth. The composts are light in weight and easy to manage and all the separate ingredients can be stored for considerable periods before mixing. The main disadvantage is that the safe level of nutrients is lower because of the loss of the loam's buffering effect, and therefore earlier feeding is necessary. This problem has recently been overcome with the introduction of slow-release fertilizers in the form of resin-coated beads that are mixed in with the compost. The beads contain the major plant nutrients in highly soluble form and controlled amounts diffuse steadily through the coating. These composts will feed the plant for many months. The rate of release of the nutrients is dependent only on soil temperature. Higher temperatures give a faster release rate, so the plants receive the maximum amount of nutrients in summer, when they are growing rapidly. Conversely, low temperatures slow down nutrient release so that in winter, when plants are resting, only minimal quantities are available to them. As the plants grow they must be moved on into larger pots to ensure that greater reserves of nutrient are available. Not all loamless composts have these fertilizers incorporated, so inquire carefully before purchasing.

Whatever kind of compost is used, it is vital that it is free from disease organisms and weed seeds and it is therefore important not to incorporate unsterilized materials such as garden soil. Garden compost produced by rotting down discarded vegetable matter is also entirely unsuitable.

A good compost provides the roots with anchorage, a reserve of water, air, nutrients, and good drainage. Plants should be potted so that the compost is in close contact with the roots, but only just firmly enough to anchor the plant in an upright position. It is important not to compress the compost so that too much air is excluded – a certain amount is a requirement for growth. Young cuttings should preferably be potted into small, approximately 3in (8cm), pots because these will dry out fairly quickly and losses due to over-watering will be reduced. Care must be taken to handle young cuttings by their leaves when potting because any bruising of the stem may cause the plant to fail.

The term 'potting-on' is used to describe the transfer of a plant from the pot in which it is growing to a larger one. This should be done as soon as the roots of the plant have grown to fill the ball of compost and are beginning to emerge from the bottom of the pot. The plant can be removed from its original pot by supporting it in an inverted position and sharply tapping the pot rim on the edge of the greenhouse bench. The pot to which it is transferred should be about $1\frac{1}{2}$in (4cm) larger in diameter. A sufficiently thick layer of compost is placed in the pot so that the surface of the original soil ball will be slightly below the final level of compost (see diagram on right). More compost is added round the edges and settled into position with a few sharp taps on the outside of the pot. A space should be left between the top of the compost and the rim of the pot, so that sufficient water can be applied at each watering to soak the entire root ball. Potting-on should be carried out at regular intervals until a 7in (18cm) pot is reached. A pot of this size is usually large enough to ensure that in hot weather daily watering will suffice and it will keep most fuchsia cultivars growing and flowering well. Plants kept

A young cutting should initially be potted into a 3in (8cm) pot and then potted-on into a larger container when the roots fill the soil ball.

from previous years will probably need a larger final pot, between 9in (23cm) and 12in (30cm) in diameter, depending on the vigour of the particular cultivar.

Watering

After potting, the plant should be watered only lightly. Heavy watering will displace air from the compost and cause the roots to die – a fate to which young fuchsias are particularly susceptible. After the initial watering, spraying the plant with clean rainwater will help it to remain turgid while the root system is establishing.

Subsequent watering should take place when the compost has become dry, and preferably just before the plant begins to wilt. Sometimes, in very hot weather, the surface of the compost will appear to be dry although the compost underneath is still damp. With experience, lifting the pot to test its weight will quickly reveal how damp the compost really is. It is a worthwhile exercise to fill pots with compost, and add different amounts of water to them for trial against a pot full of dry compost. When a fuchsia has become well established and the roots are filling the compost, the plant will require frequent watering.

Most of the water supplied to a plant is taken up by the roots and passes up through the plant to be given off by the leaves and flowers. In hot sunny weather the rate of this transpiration is greater and plants will require watering more frequently. In the summer a plant in direct sunshine may wilt even though the root ball is still wet; this is because the plant is losing water from its leaves faster than the roots can take it up. A plant in this condition should not be watered again but should be shaded from the heat of the sun. (During the first bright days of spring the soft young growth is particularly susceptible to wilting from this cause but the plants should nonetheless gradually be acclimatized to the full spring light because this will promote sturdy, short-jointed growth.)

In the autumn, as the temperature falls, the plants will gradually need less water but the compost should not be allowed to become excessively dry. In the winter watering should be minimal, just sufficient to keep the plants alive.

It does not matter whether mains water or rainwater is used, providing that the latter is clean and uncontaminated by pollution. Rainwater in tanks must be kept covered to keep out light and debris, otherwise it can become a source of disease. Nor does it matter whether water is applied to the top of the compost or allowed to soak up from underneath, as long as the complete root ball is thoroughly wetted. It is not advisable, however, to soak a potted fuchsia in a bucket of water, because this will leach some of the nutrients from the compost. The soil will also become saturated, excluding air, causing the roots to suffocate and die.

A plant with diseased roots will wilt because it will be unable to take up water even though the root ball is adequately moist; in these circumstances the leaves often appear dull and blue-green. Plants in this condition should be removed from their pots and the compost and dead roots carefully shaken away. The plants should then be potted back into smaller containers using fresh compost, lightly watered in, and then stood in a shaded position until the roots regrow.

Feeding
When a plant is freshly potted, its compost will provide all the nutrients required. In the early stages of growth, when the roots have filled the soil ball, it is better to pot the plant on and rely on the fresh compost to supply its needs than to use supplementary feeding. The fuchsia should only be fed when it is finally established in the pot in which it is to flower. The time that elapses between the final potting and the start of feeding will depend upon the compost used. Plants growing in soilless composts containing slow-release fertilizers will not require feeding for several months, but those in ordinary soilless composts will require feeding within four to six weeks. Fuchsias potted up using a soil-based compost will require feeding after eight to ten weeks. When the plant is in active growth, feeding should begin before the supply of nutrients in the compost is exhausted.

The main nutrients required by plants are nitrogen (N), phosphorus (P), and potassium (K). Nitrogen is required in large quantities by plants and is taken up in the form of nitrates. It is the element responsible for vegetative growth and is necessary for healthy leaves and stems. Phosphorus (phosphate) aids root formation, the production of fruit and flowers, and seedling growth. Potassium (potash) produces strong, sturdy, healthy plants and assists the formation of flowers and fruit. Plants also require smaller quantities of other elements such as iron and magnesium, together with minute quantities of micro-nutrients (trace elements), but these are usually adequately supplied by the potting compost.

Plant foods are available in many different forms. Slow-release granular fertilizers can be stirred into the surface of the compost around the base of the plant; the nutrient is released and distributed throughout the soil ball when the plant is watered. Feeding spikes are available that can be pushed into the compost and which slowly release nutrients over a period of time. Special feeding mats, placed in a saucer under the pot, release nutrients when the plant is watered from the base. However, the most popular and cheapest form of feeding is with liquid or solid fertilizers diluted or dissolved with water and applied as part of the general watering routine. The type of fertilizer used varies with the time of year. In the spring, autumn, and winter, when light levels are low, the nitrogen requirement is less than in the summer. During these seasons fuchsias benefit from a feed with a high potassium content to encourage short-jointed, sturdy growth and the formation of flowers. In summer, when relatively more nitrogen is required to maintain healthy green growth, it is advisable to change to a feed with a higher nitrogen content. This will also help to prolong the flowering period, because new flower buds are produced at the tips of the stems and a shortage of nitrogen greatly slows down vegetative growth and the subsequent production of flowers. Nitrogen shortage is often the cause of intermittent flowering.

In many countries, the law requires that the relative amounts of nitrogen, phosphorus, and potassium be shown on fertilizer packages. The analysis is often given in the form of a simple ratio or as a ratio of the percentages of each element present. The fertilizer for spring, autumn, and winter application should be rich in potassium, so either a 1:1:2 or 1:1:3 NPK fertilizer should be suitable. Tomatoes have a high demand for potassium, so tomato fertilizers will also be satisfactory for fuchsias. During the summer months the fertilizer should have a higher nitrogen content and a formulation of 2:1:1 or 3:1:1 NPK will be suitable. Fertilizers sold for foliage house plants usually come into this category and will give flowering plants an extra boost during the height of the flowering period.

The phosphorus content of a supplementary fertilizer is not critical – phosphorus is not leached from the potting compost as easily as potassium or nitrogen. The phosphate supplied by the compost is often sufficient for an extended period of growth. However, in hard-water areas, phosphates combine with the salts dissolved in the water to form white deposits, often visible around the top of the pot. In high concentrations a build up of this deposit may affect the growth of the plant. If such unsightly white deposits are seen, fertilizers without phosphates, such as a 2:0:1 or 1:0:2 formulation can be used.

The amount of fertilizer used and its frequency of application will depend on the current rate of plant growth and this is related to how often the plants need to be watered. In the summer when plants are growing well they will, on average, need watering every day and it will be necessary to feed them once a week. An alternative approach is to use 1/7th of the usual recommended rate of feed in the daily water. One advantage of this method is that plants are most unlikely to receive an excessive amount of feed at any time. An excessively strong fertilizer solution can result in damage to the plant roots and cause the plant to wilt. In severe cases the plant roots will rot and the whole plant will collapse and die. It is therefore vitally important to follow the manufacturer's instructions when diluting the fertilizer for use. During the other seasons, because watering will be less frequent, the need to feed will also be reduced. Therefore, if watering is taking place every other day, feeeding will only be necessary once a fortnight and in winter, if the plants are not growing, they will probably not require feeding at all.

It is important to anticipate the need for feeding because plants that have had their progress checked will take some time to recover and begin to make new growth. As a general rule, when the compost is becoming exhausted, any formulation of plant feed will be better than none at all, but obviously the best results will only be obtained by following the correct procedures.

Propagation

Fuchsias from cuttings The four main requirements for a good propagating environment are air, light, warmth, and moisture. Air provides oxygen and carbon dioxide without which plants cannot grow. Light is necessary for photosynthesis and lack of it causes weak and thin growth. Photosynthesis ceases altogether at temperatures below 50°F (10°C) and for rapid rooting a temperature of 60–68°F (16–20°C) is necessary. When additional heating is required it is more effective to heat the rooting compost than the surrounding air, and this is most easily achieved by heating cables or a proprietary propagator. A high level of humidity is required to prevent transpiration; cuttings that wilt excessively will usually fail to root. One of the cardinal rules of propagation is that only the strongest, healthiest cuttings should be used.

Although fuchsia cuttings root readily at almost any time of year, the easiest to propagate are the soft-tip cuttings produced in the spring. At this time of the year, when new growth is made, no flower buds should be present and the stems are soft and green. A cutting approximately 1½in (4cm) long is taken from the growing tip using a sharp, clean knife or razor blade. At no stage in the procedure should the cuttings be allowed to wilt – if there is any delay between taking the cuttings and planting, they may be immersed in a bowl of water. The lower leaves are removed and the base of the cutting is dipped into a hormone rooting powder and inserted into a sterile rooting medium. There are many composts or peat blocks especially formulated for sowing seeds or rooting cuttings and one of these should be used. Potting composts are not suitable, they have too high a concentration of nutrients, which inhibits root formation.

The cuttings should be lightly watered in, preferably with water containing a fungicide such as benomyl to prevent botrytis, and placed in the enclosed humid environment of a propagator. If a propagator is not available the tray or pot of cuttings should be enclosed in a large polythene bag (allowing them plenty of air) and placed in a warm, light place. On bright days the propagator will need quite heavy shading, because the temperature can rise very rapidly in an enclosed environment. The cuttings will root in one to two weeks. Their appearance changes quite noticeably at this stage, from a dull bluish-green to a much brighter and paler colour. The propagator should then gradually be ventilated to acclimatize the cuttings to a lower humidity before they are transferred to the open greenhouse. After another two or three days they should be ready for potting up.

When a fuchsia comes into bloom its hormonal balance alters. One consequence of this is that cuttings taken from fuchsias that have begun to flower will not root as readily as those from non-flowering plants. Cuttings taken from flowering plants should be about 3–4in (8–10cm) long and trimmed to just below a leaf node, where the concentration of natural rooting hormone is strongest. The

A soft-tip cutting, about 1½in (4cm) long, taken in the spring.

A semi-ripe cutting, 3–4in (8–10cm) long, taken from a flowering plant and trimmed just below a leaf node.

A woody cutting taken in autumn or winter. A side shoot, 6–7in (15–18cm) long, is pulled off the parent plant with a heel attached. The heel is trimmed before insertion.

lower leaves are removed and also any flower buds, because these would weaken the cutting by taking food from it to continue their growth. The cuttings are then dipped in hormone rooting powder and planted in the same way as soft-tip cuttings. They will take two to four weeks to root or sometimes longer, depending on the woodiness of the cutting. These cuttings are normally taken in the summer when the ambient temperature is sufficient to root them without supplementary heating. Summer-rooted cuttings have advantages for the amateur grower: they do not demand any expensive equipment and are a convenient size to overwinter but will produce large specimen plants for flowering the next year.

Cuttings taken in autumn or winter are hard and woody and more difficult to root. They should be about 6–7in (15–18cm) long and pulled off the parent plant with a heel attached (see diagram on page 23). The cutting is prepared by trimming the heel and removing the lower leaves and any flower buds. It is then treated with hormone rooting powder and planted as described previously. Even with bottom heat, these cuttings will be slow to root. They must be overwintered at a temperature between 46–50°F (8–10°C) or they will not survive. Active growth may not start until the following spring.

Producing new fuchsias Some new varieties of fuchsia have occurred spontaneously as sports, – that is, as mutants differing in some way, commonly in the colour of their leaves or flowers, from their parent plants. Sports can occur from time to time in any fuchsia collection. One example is 'Hampshire Blue', which is a pale-flowered sport of 'Carmel Blue'. The lighter-coloured flowers were first noticed on one branch of an otherwise normal plant and a new cultivar, retaining the desired coloured variation, was raised from a cutting taken from this branch. This was marketed under the name 'Hampshire Blue' to conform to the requirements of the International Rules of Nomenclature that an appropriate part of the name of the parent plant should be included in the name of the sport.

More usually, though, new fuchsias are raised from seed, either purchased from a seed company or selected by the hybridizer from plants that have been naturally pollinated. Serious hybridizers should have definite ideas on the characteristics they wish to introduce into the new plant and should select the parents with this aim in mind. Some knowledge of the quite complex laws of heredity is useful, but the usual starting point is simply to select two parent plants each of which has one of the characteristics that are required to be combined in the offspring. These may be, for example, the flower colour of one parent and the type of growth of the other. 'La Campanella' is self branching and very free flowering and has been used extensively as a mother plant in the production of new cultivars with a similar habit but different flower colour; 'Harry Gray' and 'Westminster Chimes' are two of them.

When making a deliberate cross, a careful procedure must be followed to exclude the possibility of self-fertilization or cross-pollination by insects. Select a bud that is just about to open, roll back the sepals to reveal the pollen-bearing anthers, and carefully remove them with a pair of sharp scissors. At this stage the stigma is immature and fertilization cannot take place, but the point at which it becomes receptive is difficult to predict and this operation will prevent self-fertilization. To protect a plant against unwanted insect pollination the flower should be enclosed in a paper bag or the whole plant placed in an insect-proof cage. In a few days the stigma will ripen and become sticky and pollen taken from the other parent plant will adhere to it. It is still advisable to protect the stigma against subsequent insect pollination. The seeds should be extracted when the fruit becomes dark red and soft. The small fruit should be split in half and the centre pulp spread on to some newspaper, which will also absorb much of the juice. The seeds are large enough to be picked off of the paper individually and should preferably be sown at once. Use a good quality seed compost and cover them with a very thin layer of compost passed through a fine sieve. Lightly water them in and germination should occur within fourteen days at a temperature of 60–66°F (16–19°C). Commonly, however, only about a third will germinate. The seedlings are pricked out when large enough to handle and grown on in the usual manner. Seedlings that are very similar to their parents and show little or no worthwhile improvements should not be named. It is fascinating to watch the development of the seedlings and the formation of the first flowers. With some experience and a lot of luck an exceptional seedling may be produced that is worthy of registering with the American Fuchsia Society.

TRAINING FUCHSIAS

Bushes

The bush is the most common shape for trained fuchsias. A young cutting is grown on until it has developed four to six pairs of leaves and the growing tip is then removed. This is referred to as 'pinching' or 'stopping'. Side shoots will then develop from the leaf axils and these are pinched when they have developed three pairs of leaves. For most decorative purposes this amount of shaping will suffice – each time the plant is stopped, flowering will be delayed by eight to fourteen weeks. As the plants grow larger, it is necessary to support the main stems with canes and ties; these will eventually be concealed by the foliage.

Show plants require more attention to detail and the characteristics of each individual cultivar will dictate the exact amount of shaping and training necessary. Many exhibitors will pinch out the growing tip of a young cutting when three pairs of leaves have formed and subsequently at every two pairs of leaves. However to allow sufficient time for the plant to come into flower all pinching should cease eight to ten weeks before the show for a single-flowered cultivar and ten to fourteen weeks for a double.

Standards

Standards should always be grown from the strongest cuttings available. Those cuttings that produce three leaves at each node are a particularly good choice because they will subsequently produce a nicely balanced head. A young cutting is potted up in the usual manner and a short cane inserted close to it. As the cutting grows it is tied to the cane at approximately 3–4in (8–10cm) intervals. All side shoots are removed as soon as they are large enough to handle, by holding them between the thumb and forefinger close to the main stem and pulling them away sideways. To avoid damage to the main stem, side shoots longer than 3in (8cm) are best cut away using a sharp knife or razor blade.

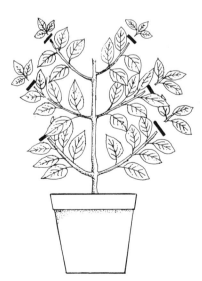

At this stage the young standard is usually referred to as a whip. The whip should be grown rapidly to the desired height without check, changing the supporting cane as necessary. It is often easier to grow the whips during the winter months when the plants are not flowering, but this is only possible in a

Opposite above: a young plant has its growing tip removed to encourage the development of side shoots.

Right: a whip's side shoots should be removed as soon as they are large enough to handle.

Far right: when the head of the standard has formed, the leaves can be removed from the main stem.

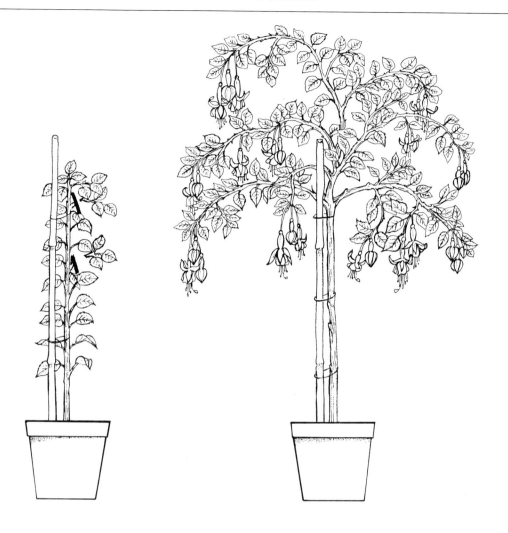

Opposite below: to produce a well-shaped, bushy plant, side shoots are stopped when they have developed three pairs of leaves.

heated greenhouse with a minimum temperature of 55°F (13°C). Above this minimum temperature plants continue to photosynthesize and grow. Any check in growth from low temperatures or an inadequate supply of nutrients will result in deformities in the stem. The growing tip is removed when the plant has reached the required height, leaving the shoots from the top four sets of leaves to develop into the head. A table standard measures 10–17in (25–43cm) from the top of the compost to the lower branches of the head, a half standard measures 18–29in (46–74cm), and a full standard 30–42in (76–107cm). These are British Fuchsia Society guidelines for exhibiting, but for decorative purposes standards may, of course, be trained to any height the grower pleases. Until the head is well formed the leaves growing up the main stem should be retained for as long as possible to produce food required for growth. The side shoots are pinched after developing four pairs of leaves and further shaping is the same as for bush fuchsias. When fully grown the size of the head will, to some extent, be dependent upon the cultivar chosen, but it should be in scale with the height of the plant. In subsequent years, it will be necessary to maintain this balance by pruning. The head of the fuchsia should be tied into the central cane and all the main branches supported with string, otherwise the weight of the flowers may cause them to break. As the head continues to grow the supporting string will gradually be concealed by the foliage.

Any plants that are stood out of doors should be staked very firmly and the top of the stem inside the head secured to the stake. In the autumn the head should be trimmed back by two-thirds, the old compost shaken off of the roots, and the plant potted back into a smaller container. Standards, even of recognized hardy cultivars, may be killed back to ground level in severe weather and should be kept frost free during the winter. The following spring, when growth recommences, the standard can be potted on as necessary.

The above method describes the most usual way of growing standard fuchsias, but when the stem is soft it is very amenable to training and it is possible to produce standards with corkscrew stems by twisting them, as they grow, around the supporting cane. Similarly if three cuttings are potted together, they can be plaited as they grow to give a 'plaited standard'. The cuttings should be chosen with great care to be as identical as possible or they will tend to grow at different rates and make training difficult.

Pillars

Pillars, also known as 'cordons', are grown in a similar manner to standards, but the side shoots are not removed. Instead, they are all trimmed to the same length. The resulting shape should be a perfect cylinder, covered in flowers. This can be a difficult shape to perfect as the lower and upper branches vary in vigour and grow at very different rates.

Espaliers and fans

These once very popular forms are rarely seen today because they take up a lot of room space and often demand a heated greenhouse.

To produce an espalier a young plant is grown up a central cane and the side shoots trained as laterals along horizontal wire supports placed approximately 6in (15cm) apart. Any lateral shoots that do not coincide with the wires are removed. Providing a suitable cultivar is chosen, the height of the main stem and the length of the laterals is limited only by the space available. When they are stopped the lateral growths produce secondary shoots that bear the blooms and the result should be a flat wall of flowers.

The fan shape is achieved by stopping a young plant after it has produced three pairs of leaves. The side shoots produced are tied to individual small canes and stopped again after producing three pairs of leaves. The most vigorous shoot from each break is tied to a suitable support to form the flattened radials of a fan and any unwanted shoots are removed. This process is continued until the fan has reached the required size, but in the meantime the tips of the side shoots produced on the radials should be pinched out. At this stage the plant should be allowed to flower. Espalier and fan-trained shapes are an excellent alternative method of displaying trailing cultivars that would normally be grown in hanging baskets.

Pyramids

The pyramid fuchsia is shaped like a Christmas tree, wide at the base and tapering to the crown. It is formed by planting a vigorous young cutting and growing it up a cane to a height of 9–12in (23–30cm), retaining all the side shoots. The growing tip is pinched out and the most vigorous side shoot produced from near the top is tied to the cane to act as a new leader. This action encourages the growth of the lateral branches and is necessary to achieve the required shape. This process is repeated every 9–12in (23–30cm), until the plant has reached the required height, when the growing tip is finally removed.

All the major side shoots will need to be well supported by canes pushed into the pot at an angle of 45° to the central cane and smaller branches can be tied up with string. In its first year the plant reaches the required height and the side shoots are grown to the desired width. During the first winter pruning is confined to improving the overall shape and this framework of mature wood gives a good basis for fresh growth in the spring. However all the main branches will still need to be supported or the extra weight of flowers may cause them to break from the main stem.

Hanging baskets

This is a most effective way of displaying fuchsias that have a naturally lax or trailing habit of growth.

Hanging baskets are available made from galvanized or plastic-coated wire, or constructed entirely of plastic. Plastic baskets often have a built-in drip tray, which facilitates watering in a dry summer, but in a wet summer the tray may stay constantly full of water thus saturating the compost and causing the plant to fail. Wire baskets are available in larger sizes than plastic ones and vigorous cultivars benefit from the extended root run and greater reservoir of nutrients. Before being filled with compost, wire baskets have to be lined with moss, polythene, or one of the modern proprietary liners. To prevent the basket from rolling while being planted it can be supported on a bowl or bucket. The number of plants necessary to fill a basket will depend on its size and their size and vigour. One plant from a 4in (10cm) pot will fill a small basket, but three of these plants or five from 3in (8cm) pots will be needed to fill a 12in (30cm) basket. Very lax

cultivars often require an extra plant to fill in the centre of the basket. Different cultivars should not be planted in the same basket, because they will have different rates of growth and the resulting effect will be ugly and unbalanced. Very vigorous cultivars will also quickly outgrow and overwhelm weaker ones. Lax cultivars such as 'Texas Longhorn', 'Trail Blazer', and 'Rough Silk' should be hung up high, because they never seem adequately to cover the top of the basket and the flowers are produced at the ends of the long trailing stems. Those cultivars with compact growth tend to produce a more ball-shaped basket that is seen to advantage from a lower viewpoint, because the flowers are produced mainly over the top and sides. Wire baskets have the additional advantage that small plants can be inserted in the bottom between the wires to complete the effect.

Baskets for outside decoration should be planted up as early as possible so that they are well established when the time comes to harden them off for hanging outdoors. Plants suddenly placed outside in bright sunshine can suffer a severe check to growth, with the foliage becoming bronzed and flowering delayed. The plants are initially stood outside in a shaded, sheltered spot, because the change in humidity and buoyancy of the air will affect the rate of transpiration. For the first seven days they should be returned to the greenhouse at night, but after that they can remain permanently outside provided the weather is suitable. After another two days they can be moved to a more sunny position.

Exhibiting fuchsias

When entering a competitive show, it is most important to read the schedule carefully, because *all* specifications must be carefully adhered to. Should the pot size stipulated in a class be 5in (12·5cm), then using a pot size of $4\frac{3}{4}$in (12cm) or $5\frac{1}{4}$in (13cm) will result in disqualification. Similarly, if the schedule specifies a hardy cultivar then it must be one recognized by the authority under whose rules the show is organized and not one that has proved hardy in the grower's own garden.

Some cultivars are much easier than others to grow well for exhibition and each exhibitor will have his or her own favourites. The cultivars that are compact in growth, self-branching, and very free flowering have obvious advantages as show plants. The general cultivation of show plants is basically the same as that of those grown purely for decoration. Normally, two-year-old plants are used, growing a well-shaped framework in the first year and in the second year concentrating on good healthy foliage followed by prolific flowering. Most shows are held in the summer months because this is the natural flowering time for fuchsias. During the late spring and early summer, when the plant starts to bloom the prospective show plant should be fed with a high-nitrogen feed (2:0:1) to promote maximum growth and continued flower-bud production.

The plant may be shaped and stopped during this time but this process should cease, for a single-flowered cultivar, eight to ten weeks before the show date or, for a double, ten to fourteen weeks. Any flower buds that will open and drop before the required show date should be removed as soon as they are large enough to handle, to encourage the plant to produce even more buds. About a month before the show the feed should be changed to a high-potash formulation to harden up the growth and improve the colour and substance of the flowers.

Fuchsia stems are extremely brittle and the flowers easily bruised, so great care should be taken when transporting a plant to the show. A few extra supporting canes that can be removed on arrival are a good idea. To prevent the movement of large blooms and subsequent damage, some growers wrap newspaper or muslin around the plant to provide some measure of support. The pot should be stood in a cardboard box approximately the same height as the pot and carefully packed around with newspaper to prevent it falling over. It is best to transport a basket by hanging it from a support, with ties to prevent it from swinging, however if this is not possible it should be packed in a cardboard box with the stems allowed to trail over the edges.

Large standards are difficult to transport in a car but seem to travel best in the front with the passenger seat partially reclined. The head of the fuchsia should carefully be guided back over the reclined seat, which also supports its stem. The pot can be prevented from rolling by supporting it in a cardboard box and packing it firmly with newspaper. Further support can be given to the stem by looping a length of soft rope around it and tying the end to opposite sides of the vehicle. The head should be positioned at such an angle that it does not touch any part of the car. The supporting cane of the standard may become loose in transit so that it no longer stands upright; this can be avoided by pushing a few small stones into the compost around the supporting cane.

Where two exhibits are of similar merit, good presentation may often be a deciding factor in determining the prizewinner. So pots should be cleaned and any loose compost brushed from the tabling.

A well-grown fuchsia, free of pests and disease and at its peak of perfection, is an ideal show plant. Therefore, it is essential to keep records from one year to another so that improvements can be made in feeding, stopping, timing, and other procedures. It is not easy to win top prizes but everyone has to start somewhere, and experience can be gained only by entering shows and making critical comparisons.

PROSPERITY
Gadsby, UK, 1970
Large, double blooms that are
freely produced on strong
upright growth. The tube and
sepals are red and the corolla
a very pale pink, almost
white, heavily veined with
red. A lovely, hardy garden
plant.

GOLDEN LENA
Unknown, UK, 1978
A sport of 'Lena' with variegated green and gold foliage. The tube and sepals are pink and the corolla rose-magenta. The medium-sized, semi-double blooms are very freely produced. This cultivar is as hardy as 'Lena' but not as vigorous. In common with most variegated foliage fuchsias, the young plants are susceptible to botrytis.

NELLIE NUTTALL
Roe, UK, 1977
Small, single flowers that are produced in profusion and held erect. The tube and sepals are bright red and the creamy white corolla is veined with red. The growth is upright and very compact. An outstanding cultivar for a small-pot class in a show.

CANDLELIGHT
Waltz, USA, 1959
Large, full, double flower (above). The tube and sepals are white and the sepals are flushed with pink on the underside. The corolla is deep lilac-purple, flushed with rose at the base of the petals. The corolla fades to a deep rose with age. The habit is very strong and upright, and the very thick stems produced are typical of this cultivar.

FUCHSIA BOLIVIANA ALBA
The long, single flowers (right) are carried in clusters and are followed by attractive berries. The tube and sepals are white, although the underside of the sepals is flushed with pink. The flaring petals are bright red. This is the white-tubed variant of *Fuchsia boliviana*, a species that was originally discovered in Bolivia (as the name commemorates) but is now the most widely naturalized fuchsia. There are also several varieties of *Fuchsia boliviana* that vary only in the length of the tube – those plants with a tube length of 2–2½in (5–6cm) have been described as *Fuchsia boliviana v. luxurians*.

BABY PINK
Soo Yun, USA, 1976
Double with medium-sized blooms (left). The tube and sepals are pale pink. The full corolla is an even paler soft pink. The growth is very compact and trailing. A very free-flowering plant suitable for a hanging pot or table standard.

CORSAIR

Kennett, USA, 1965

Large, double flowers. The tube and sepals are white. The corolla is purple splashed heavily with white, particularly on the outer petals. The flowers are most unusual but not very freely produced. The growth is trailing and unless frequently pinched forms long untidy branches.

CELADORE

Hall, UK, 1981

The large, double flowers are a deep candy pink and very freely produced. The growth is lax and cascading. This is an easy cultivar to grow and its cuttings root well.
A beautiful plant for a hanging basket or weeping standard.

SONATA
Tiret, USA, 1960
Large, double blooms. The tube and sepals are pink and the very full corolla creamy white. The growth is upright and bushy but rather brittle and needs supporting. This cultivar is not as easy to grow well as the similarly coloured 'Nancy Lou' (see page 76).

FLIRTATION WALTZ
Waltz, USA, 1962
Medium-to-large, double flowers. The tube and sepals are creamy white tinged with pink and the corolla is a soft powder pink. The flowers are borne in profusion on stiff, upright growth, although the stems are somewhat brittle. The foliage is grey-green and a lovely foil for the pastel flowers. Unfortunately the flowers mark and bruise easily, which can cause problems on the showbench.

R.A.F.
Garson, USA, 1942
Double. The tube and sepals
are red and the corolla a pale
dusky pink veined with red.
The quite large flowers are
produced in profusion on
bushy, compact growth. An
excellent show plant that is
easy to grow and train.
Similar to 'Fascination' (see
pages 64–5), but easier to
grow well.

COTTON CANDY
Tiret, USA, 1962
Large, double blooms in a
very soft shade of palest pink.
The sepals recurve and twist
away from the full corolla.
The growth is upright and
bushy. 'Cotton Candy'
requires very little training to
make a lovely bush and also
makes a very pretty standard.

BROOKWOOD JOY
Gilbert, UK, 1983
Medium-to-large, full double blooms (above). The white tube and sepals are flushed with very pale pink. The corolla is deep blue splashed heavily with pink at the base of the petals. The growth is bushy but lax and trails under the weight of blooms produced. One of the most attractive recent introductions.

PEPPERMINT STICK
Walker & Jones, USA, 1950
Large, double flowers (right) that are very freely produced on strong upright growth. The tube and sepals are red and the full corolla purple and deep pink. The inner petals are purple and the outer petals are deep pink streaked with purple at the edges. A superb cultivar for show work that can be trained as a standard, pillar, or pyramid.

HAMPSHIRE BEAUTY
Clark, UK, 1987
Single (above). The tube and sepals are white tinged with green. The corolla is pale blue and the petals are edged with a deeper shade of blue. The foliage is variegated in gold and green and very beautiful. The growth is upright, very compact, and bushy. A sport of 'Belvoir Beauty' (see page 108).

LADY THUMB
Roe, UK, 1966

Small, semi-double flowers that are very freely produced. The tube and sepals are deep pink and the corolla creamy white with red veining. The small, dark green foliage is borne on upright, bushy, and very compact growth. A beautiful show cultivar for a small-pot class, 'Lady Thumb' is a sport of 'Tom Thumb' (see page 137).

LAVENDER KATE
Holmes, UK, 1970
Large, double flower. The large buds are white with a faint tinge of pink but as the buds open the tube and sepals deepen to pink. The corolla is a soft lavender-blue. The leaves are dark green and the habit is upright and bushy.

HIDCOTE BEAUTY
Unknown, UK, 1949
Medium-sized, single flowers. The tube and sepals are cream and the corolla a soft salmon orange flushed with cream at the base of the petals. The leaves are pale green and the growth upright and bushy. An easy cultivar to train for show work, it is particularly attractive when grown as a standard.

MR A. HUGGETT
Unknown, UK, *c*.1930
Small, single flowers that are produced in profusion. The short tube and sepals are red and the corolla pale mauve with a deeper mauve edge to the petals. The compact growth is upright and bushy and the leaves are small. It makes a superb show plant. Hardy.

FUCHSIA DENTICULATA
A species fuchsia (left) with long, reddish-pink tube and sepals tipped with green. The corolla is bright orange deepening to red. An extremely vigorous plant that makes a lovely specimen. It is synonymous with
F. grandiflora, *F. serratifolia* and *F. tasconiflora*.

GOLD BROCADE
Tabraham, UK, 1976
Large, single flower (above). The tube and sepals are red and the corolla is mauve, fading to pink with age. The foliage is gold-green with pronounced red veining but the leaves mature to pale green. The growth is upright and bushy.

CLOVERDALE JEWEL
Gadsby, UK, 1974
Semi-double (left and
opposite). The tube and sepals
are deep pink and the corolla
light blue. The petals are
flushed with white at the base
and veined with deep pink.
The habit is upright and very
bushy and this cultivar makes
a beautiful specimen bush
with very little stopping.

ROYAL VELVET
Waltz, USA, 1962
Large, double flowers (above) that are borne in profusion. The tube and sepals are crimson and the corolla deep purple, although the bases of the outer petals are heavily splashed with red. The growth is vigorous, upright, and self-branching. This is one of the easiest cultivars to grow well and it makes a fine show plant in any form except a hanging basket.

RADCLIFFE BEDDER
Roe, UK, 1980
Single (right). The tube and fully recurved sepals are light red. The corolla is deep blue-purple veined with red and the bases of the petals are flushed with pink. The growth is upright and very vigorous. A reliable, hardy garden plant that is very free flowering.

ROSE OF DENMARK
Reimers, USA, 1864
Medium-sized blooms that are
either single or semi-double.
In the bud stage the tube and
sepals are white, but as the
flower opens they are flushed
with pale pink. The corolla is
a beautiful shade of rose-pink
and the petal edges are a
slightly deeper shade. The
growth is very bushy but
quite lax and this beautiful
cultivar is easily trained to
make a lovely standard or
hanging basket.

CAROLINE
Miller, UK, 1967
Large, single flowers that
eventually open almost flat.
The tube and sepals are
cream, heavily flushed with
pink. The initially bell-like
corolla is a pale violet-blue
shading to pale pink at the
base of the petals. The mass of
flower is carried on upright
growth and this cultivar
makes a lovely bush.

CITY OF ADELAIDE
Richardson, Australia, 1986
Very large, full, double flower.
The tube is white striped with
green and the sepals are
white on the upper surface
but flushed with pink on the
underside. The corolla is deep
violet maturing to magenta
and the base of the petals is
white. The green foliage is
borne on strong trailing
growth. A late-flowering
cultivar.

55

MARGARET

Wood, UK, 1937 or 1943
Semi-double or double flowers
(opposite) that are quite large
for a hardy cultivar. The very
short, bulbous tube and
recurving sepals are red. The
corolla is blue-purple fading
to magenta and the petals are
splashed and veined with red
at the base. The growth is
upright, bushy, and rather
spreading.

LOEKY

de Graaff, Netherlands, 1981
Medium-to-large, single
flowers (left) that open almost
flat. The tube and sepals are
red and the corolla a pale
lavender-rose. The growth is
upright and very bushy. The
blooms are borne in profusion
and stand out well from the
plant. An extremely good
fuchsia, which will make a
fine show plant.

COUNTESS OF ABERDEEN
Forbes, UK, 1888
Small, single flowers (right).
The tube and outer sepals are
greenish white but the
underside of the sepals is
tinged with palest pink. The
corolla is very pale pink,
almost white, but when
grown in full sun the flowers
become distinctly pink. The
growth is very upright and
bushy but requires frequent
stopping when it is young if it
is to make a good show
specimen.

GAY FANDANGO
Nelson, USA, 1951
Double (opposite). The tube
and sepals are pink and the
corolla a deep rose-magenta.
The petals of the corolla are
tiered, making the large
flower appear long. An
extremely vigorous, lax
grower that requires frequent
pinching as a young plant.
The flowers are carried on the
long, trailing growth. A good
cultivar for a hanging basket.

58

HAMPSHIRE BLUE
Clark, UK, 1983
Single (right and opposite below left). The tube and sepals are white, flushed and veined with pink and the corolla is a soft silver-blue. The medium-sized flowers are very freely produced on strong, upright growth. This cultivar makes an excellent show plant and is particularly attractive when grown as a standard. It is a pastel-flowered sport of 'Carmel Blue'.

CHANCE ENCOUNTER
Schneider, USA, 1980
Tiny, single flower of the Encliandra type (far left). The long tube, sepals, and petals are bright pink and the sepals are tipped with white. The fine fern-like foliage is also very small and dark green. The growth is lax and spreading. An unusual cultivar for a hanging basket or as a hardy plant in a sheltered part of the garden.

COLLINGWOOD
Niederholzer, USA, 1945
Large, double blooms (left). The tube and reflexing sepals are pink. The corolla is creamy white and the petals are veined with pink at the base. The upright growth is very vigorous and the foliage dark green. The strong stems are easily trained as a standard, pillar, or pyramid.

FUCHSIA PROCUMBENS
A prostrate, trailing species (left) first discovered growing in the sand on beaches in New Zealand. The tiny flowers are held upright. The tube is yellow and the recurved sepals are green and purple. There is no corolla, but the red stamens bear bright blue pollen. The flowers are followed by quite large plum-like fruits that are equally attractive. The tiny leaves are heart shaped and borne on slender, trailing stems. A most unusual plant that can be grown to effect on a rockery. It is synonymous with *F. prostrata*. Hardy.

61

COACHMAN
Bright, UK, *c*.1910
Single. The tube and sepals
are pale pink-orange and the
corolla bright orange with a
slight red tinge. The medium-
sized blooms are freely
produced but tend to come in
flushes. The growth is
compact and rather
spreading. A pretty cultivar
for a hanging basket. Very
similar to 'Clair de Lune' and
'Shanley'.

JEANE
Reiter, USA, 1951
Fairly small, single flowers.
The tube and sepals are cerise
and the corolla deep blue,
flushed and veined with pink
at the base of the petals. The
small leaves are bright golden
yellow and the growth
upright and very bushy. This
is a most attractive hardy
plant, the golden foliage
adding a bright splash of
colour to the border long
before the plant flowers.
Synonymous with 'Genii'.

SHARPITOR
National Trust, UK, *c.*1974
Small, single flowers. The tube is cream flushed with green and the sepals are pale pink. The corolla is a very pale lilac-pink that ages to clear pale pink. The growth is strong, upright, and bushy. The foliage is most attractively variegated in sage green and cream, with the cream being mostly round the edges of the leaves. A good, hardy cultivar.

SOPHISTICATED LADY
Martin, USA, 1964
Large, double flowers borne in profusion on long, trailing growth. The tube and long sepals are pink and the very full corolla is white. The stems are rather thin and this cultivar is best grown in a hanging basket as a two-year-old plant with the first year's wood making a supporting framework.

FASCINATION
Lemoine, France, 1905
Large, double flower. The
tube and sepals are deep rose-
red and the full corolla is soft
pink veined with rose-red.
The growth is upright and
vigorous, and this cultivar
has a high nitrogen
requirement. 'Fascination' is
synonymous with 'Emile de
Wildeman' (its original name)
and 'Rose Ballet Girl'. In the
United States it is known as
'Irwin's Great Pink'.

PINK JADE
Pybon, USA, 1958
Single. The tube and sepals
are pink and the sepals are
tipped with green. The corolla
is a glowing rose-pink with a
distinct deep rose edging to
the petals. The growth is very
compact and self-branching
and this cultivar will make a
good bush with very little
training. Unfortunately it
flowers very late in the
season.

DISPLAY
Smith, UK, 1881
A single, rose-pink flower
with the corolla being just a
slightly paler shade than the
tube and sepals. The flowers
are freely produced from early
in the season. The growth is
upright, bushy, and self-
branching; the foliage is dark
green with a faint bronze
tinge. It is one of the best
fuchsias ever produced, easily
trained into any shape for
exhibition work. An old
cultivar that was a favourite
with the Victorians and is still
popular today. Grown in the
Netherlands as 'Frau Ida
Noach'.

SATELLITE

Kennett, USA, 1965
Large, single blooms that are produced on strong, upright growth. The leaves are mid-green and form almost a rosette at the growing tip. The tube and sepals are white and the long corolla is deep magenta heavily streaked with white. This is not an easily trained cultivar and is best grown as a bush.

MOLESWORTH

Lemoine, France, 1903
Medium-to-large, double flowers that are very freely produced from early in the season. The tube and sepals are bright red and the corolla creamy white veined with red. Because the growth is extremely vigorous and trailing, 'Molesworth' will, with training, make a beautiful hanging basket.

SLEIGH BELLS
Schnabel, USA, 1954
All-white, single flowers that are produced rather late in the season. The flowers are quite large and the corolla is a beautiful bell shape. The foliage is dark green and the growth is strong and upright but arches gracefully when the plant is in flower. Young plants are susceptible to botrytis.

STRING OF PEARLS
Pacey, UK, 1976
Single to semi-double (opposite above). The tube and sepals are initially pale pink but quickly mature to a deeper shade of pink. The corolla is a pale lavender-pink with lavender veining. The flowers are very freely produced down the stems of the plant. The growth is very strong and upright but requires frequent pinching to make a good bush.

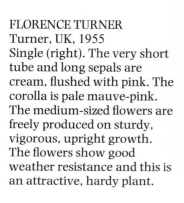

FLORENCE TURNER
Turner, UK, 1955
Single (right). The very short tube and long sepals are cream, flushed with pink. The corolla is pale mauve-pink. The medium-sized flowers are freely produced on sturdy, vigorous, upright growth. The flowers show good weather resistance and this is an attractive, hardy plant.

BOUFFANT
Tiret, USA, 1949
Single (right). The tube and sepals are cerise and the long corolla creamy white, veined with cerise at the base of the petals. The large blooms are freely produced on vigorous trailing growth. Suitable for growing as a hanging basket or weeping standard.

C. J. HOWLETT
Howlett, UK, 1911
Medium-sized single to semi-double flowers (opposite). The tube and sepals are light red tipped with green. The corolla is deep mauve but the outer petaloids are reddish purple. The growth is moderately vigorous and upright and the foliage dark green. A good, hardy cultivar.

BILLY GREEN
Unknown, UK, 1966
A single Triphylla-type bloom (left). The long-tubed flowers are salmon pink and very freely produced in clusters on the ends of the stems. The habit is very upright and bushy; the foliage is olive green but becomes lightly bronzed with maturity. Frequently seen on the showbench grown as a bush.

TRAUDCHEN BONSTEDT
Bonstedt, Germany, 1905
A Triphylla hybrid (above) with the typical long-tubed, single flowers that are borne in clusters at the growing tips. The blooms are a soft salmon and the foliage is a deep bronze. The growth is upright and self branching. This cultivar makes a most attractive bush.

CERI
Holmes, UK, 1980
Medium-sized, single flowers very freely produced. The tube, sepals, and flaring corolla are all creamy white tinged with pink but become flushed with pink unless shaded. The habit is upright and bushy but not very vigorous.

HAMPSHIRE TREASURE
Clark, UK, 1983
Double. The tube is pale creamy-pink and the sepals are a very pale salmon pink. The corolla is orange and magenta; the inner petals are predominantly magenta and the outer petals mostly orange. The medium-sized flowers are produced in profusion from early in the season until late in the autumn. The growth is vigorous, bushy, and horizontal. It is a seedling from 'Bicentennial' (see page 94) and 'Lord Lonsdale' (see page 131), and although the flowers are smaller than those of 'Bicentennial' they are more freely produced. An excellent show plant that makes a particularly lovely standard.

GOLDEN TREASURE
Carter, UK, 1860
Single. The tube and sepals are scarlet and the corolla purple-magenta. The habit is compact and bushy and the leaves are variegated in gold and green. A late-flowering cultivar that is often just grown for its beautiful foliage. Young plants are very susceptible to botrytis and the leaves are prone to scorching unless shaded.

SNOWFIRE
Stubbs, USA, 1978
Large, double blooms. The tube is deep pink and the sepals white with pink veining. The corolla is a dusky-pink and the outer petals are heavily splashed with pink and white. The dark green foliage is carried on initially upright growth that arches under the weight of the flowers.

NANCY LOU
Stubbs, USA, 1971
Double. The tube and fully recurved sepals are a clear pink and the full corolla white with slight pink veining at the base of the petals. The fairly large flowers are freely produced on strong, upright growth. This is one of the best cultivars in its colour range.

BON ACCORDE
Crousse, France, 1861
Small, single flowers held up
and out from the plant. The
tube and sepals are white and
the corolla a soft lavender
shading to white at the base
of the petals. The growth is
very strong and upright and it
requires pinching to obtain a
good specimen plant. It was
renamed in the United States
and reintroduced to Britain as
'Erecta Novelty'.

INDIAN MAID
Waltz, USA, 1962
Large, double flowers (left).
The tube and long recurving
sepals are scarlet and the
corolla is purple. The centre
and base of the petals are
veined with scarlet. The
foliage is dark green and the
habit vigorous and trailing. It
received a Certificate of Merit
from the American Fuchsia
Society in 1965.

HEIDI ANN
Smith, UK, 1969
Medium-sized, double blooms
(right). The tube and sepals
are cerise and the corolla a
pale pinkish lilac veined with
cerise. The dark green leaves
are carried on upright, very
bushy, compact growth. This
is an easy cultivar to grow
well and is a favourite with
exhibitors. Growing in the
south of England it has
survived several winters
when the temperature has
dropped to 3°F (− 16°C) and
then come into flower in late
June or early July.

A TRIAL OF HARDY FUCHSIAS

Eight varieties of hardy fuchsias on trial in a garden in the south of England (left). The rosy flowers of 'Lena' (see page 131) fill the centre left of the photograph. Around this (clockwise, starting from the bottom left-hand corner) are 'Blue Gown', 'Prosperity' (see page 33), 'Alice Hoffman' (see page 123), 'Golden Lena' (see page 34), 'Corallina' (see page 127), *Fuchsia magellanica v. macrostemma* 'Versicolor' (see page 107), and 'Mr A. Huggett' (see page 47).

ROUGH SILK
Baker, UK, 1970

Large, single flowers (above) that are freely produced. The tube is pink but the long sepals are white, flushed and veined with pink. The long corolla is a beautiful shade of deep magenta-red. The foliage is light green and the habit cascading. A beautiful fuchsia for a hanging basket.

PACQUESA
Clyne, UK, 1974
Quite large, single flowers
that are very similar in shape
to those of 'Ballet Girl'. The
tube and sepals are deep red
and the corolla white with
slight red veining. The leaves
are dark green and carried on
strong, upright stems. An
easy cultivar to grow – it is
naturally self-branching and
requires very little training to
make a good bush. An
excellent plant for summer
bedding or in a patio tub.

ABBE FARGES
Lemoine, France, 1901
Semi-double. The tube and recurving sepals are pale cerise. The corolla is pale lavender with red veining. The small flowers are very freely produced on bushy upright growth. 'Abbé Farges' is an attractive weather-resistant cultivar for permanent planting in the garden.

TENNESSEE WALTZ
Walker & Jones, USA, 1951
Large double or occasionally semi-double flowers that are very freely produced on upright, bushy growth. The tube and sepals are deep rose-pink and the corolla is lavender with splashes of pink. An easy cultivar to grow and train and recommended for beginners. Hardy.

DOLLAR PRINCESS
Lemoine, France, 1912
Small, double flowers (left and above) that are very freely produced. The tube and sepals are red and the corolla deep purple. The bases of the petals are flushed with deep pink. The leaves are dark green but fairly small. The growth is vigorous, bushy, and compact although rather spreading, particularly when planted in the garden. It is also known as 'Princess Dollar'. Hardy.

ROSE OF CASTILE
IMPROVED
Banks, UK, 1869
Single (left). The tube is
cream flushed with green and
the sepals are cream, tinged
with pink on the upper
surface and flushed with pink
on the under surface. The
corolla is a deep plum purple
with a very fine edge of red to
the petals. The growth is
strong and upright and the
medium-sized flowers are held
well out from the foliage. A
very reliable, hardy garden
plant.

GOLDEN MARINKA
Weber, USA, 1955
A variegated sport (above) of
'Marinka' (see page 132), with
single red flowers identical to
those of the parent. The
growth is lax and trailing but
not as vigorous as 'Marinka';
it does, however, make an
excellent hanging basket or
weeping standard. Not as free
flowering as 'Marinka', but
the variegated leaves are most
attractive.

LIEBRIEZ
Kohene, Germany, 1874
Small, semi-double flowers
(above) that are very freely
produced. The tube and
sepals are light red and the
corolla can be white or pale
pink on the same plant. The
petals are veined with red. In
the greenhouse the habit is
lax and spreading but in the
garden is upright and bushy.
Hardy.

TRASE
Dawson, UK, 1959
Semi-double or double (right).
The tube and sepals are deep
pink-red and the corolla a
very pale pink, veined with
deep pink. The medium-sized
blooms are very freely
produced on upright but
fairly compact growth.
Hardy.

TUTONE
Machado, USA, 1963
Large, double blooms that are
freely produced. The tube and
sepals are pink and the
corolla a deep lavender blue
splashed heavily with pink.
The growth is initially upright
but trails under the weight of
the flowers produced.
A vigorous cultivar that can
be trained as a bush,
standard, or hanging basket.

INTERLUDE
Kennett, USA, 1960
Double. The tube and sepals
of the buds are waxy white
but as the flower opens they
become flushed with pink.
The inner petals of the corolla
are deep violet-blue with a
few splashes of bright pink;
the outer petals are pink. The
growth is lax and trailing and
'Interlude' is best grown in a
hanging basket.

LADY ISOBEL BARNETT
Gadsby, UK, 1968
Medium-sized, single flowers. The tube and sepals are deep pink and the flaring corolla a very pale mauve shading to white at the base of the petals. The flowers are prolific and held semi-erect. The growth is upright and bushy and this cultivar makes an excellent show plant.

SPION KOP
Jones, UK, 1973
Medium-sized, double flowers that are very freely produced on upright, bushy growth. The tube and sepals are deep rose-pink and the corolla creamy-white veined with rose-pink. An extremely easy cultivar to grow well and highly recommended for beginners. It is easily trained as a show plant and can be relied on to flower well from early in the season.

BRUTUS
Lemoine, France, 1897
Single (left). The tube and recurving sepals are deep cerise. The corolla is deep purple with red veining at the base of the petals. The freely produced, medium-sized flowers are borne on vigorous, upright, but rather spreading branches. An easy cultivar to train for exhibition work.

GARTENMEISTER BONSTEDT
Bonstedt, Germany, 1905
A Triphylla hybrid with the typical long-tubed flowers in bright red. The flowers are freely produced on the ends of the stems, which are stiff and upright. The foliage is deep red-bronze and most attractive. This cultivar makes a good bush plant as it is naturally self-branching. It

is almost identical to 'Thalia', the only difference being a bulge in the tube of 'Gartenmeister Bonstedt'.

BICENTENNIAL
Paskesen, USA, 1976
Medium-to-large, double blooms. The tube is white with a slight orange flush and the sepals are pale salmon orange. The inner petals of the corolla are magenta and the outer petals orange with magenta streaks on the edges of the petals. The habit is semi-trailing and the foliage dark green. A beautiful cultivar for a hanging basket or standard.

MARGARET BROWN
Wood, UK, 1949
Small, single flowers that are very freely produced. The tube and sepals are deep pink and the corolla pale mauve-pink. This is an extremely vigorous, hardy cultivar that makes a good garden plant or low hedge. The light green foliage is carried on upright, bushy growth.

FIONA
Clark, UK, 1958
Large, single blooms. The tube and long, pointed sepals are white. The corolla opens deep blue but fades to a pale magenta. The flowers are carried on lax, trailing growth and 'Fiona' is best grown as a hanging basket, although it makes also an attractive weeping standard. It received an Award of Merit and the Jones Cup (1958) from the British Fuchsia Society.

DELILAH
Handley, UK, 1974
Large, double flower. The tube and sepals are basically white but flushed and veined with pink. The corolla is a deep violet-blue fading to magenta and the base of the petals is streaked with pink. The growth is upright and short-jointed and this cultivar will make a good bush.

MONSIEUR THIBAUT
Lemoine, France, 1898
Single (right and overleaf). The short, bulbous tube and sepals are waxy-red and the corolla purple. The blooms are freely produced on strong, upright growth and the leaves are dark green. An excellent, hardy garden plant which can be trained into a lovely standard or pyramid. Frequently confused with the cultivar 'Empress of Prussia' (see page 128).

MONSIEUR THIBAUT
See page 96 .

MARIN GLOW
Reedstrom, USA, 1954
Single (right). The short tube and long sepals are white and the sepals recurve at the tips. The corolla is a rich, glowing purple fading with age to magenta. The medium-sized blooms are freely produced on strong upright growth. The best flower colour is achieved when the plant is grown in the shade; if it is grown in full sunlight the flowers fade rapidly to mauve. An easy cultivar for even a beginner to grow well, because it requires very little training.

ESTELLE MARIE
Newton, USA, 1973
Small, single flowers (above) that are very freely produced. The tube and sepals are white and the sepals are tipped with green. The corolla opens pale violet-blue and matures to violet. The petals are white at the base. The dark green foliage is carried on upright but very compact growth and this cultivar will flower well in a $3\frac{1}{2}$ in (9cm) pot. A little susceptible to botrytis in the winter.

SNOWCAP
Henderson, UK, *c*.1880
Fairly small, semi-double flowers that are very freely produced on vigorous, upright, self-branching growth. The tube and sepals are bright red and the corolla white veined very slightly with red. An easy cultivar to grow well, and it should be in every beginner's collection.

ORANGE DROPS
Martin, USA, 1963
Single. The tube and sepals are pale orange and the corolla is deep orange. The growth is compact, bushy, and horizontal. The foliage is a light sage green. With suitable training this cultivar can be grown as a bush, hanging basket, or standard.

LADY KATHLEEN SPENCE
Ryle, UK, 1974
Medium-sized, single flowers.
The tube and sepals are white
flushed with pink. The corolla
is a soft lavender-blue that
fades to a pale lilac. The
growth is upright and bushy.
A fine, free-flowering fuchsia
that was, in 1976, the first
cultivar to receive the British
Fuchsia Society's Gold
Certificate of Merit.

EVENSONG
Colville, UK, 1967
Single (right). The tube is
white flushed with pink and
the sepals white and flushed
at the base with deep pink.
The sepals recurve back to
cover the tube, exposing the
white, bell-like corolla. The
medium-sized flowers are
freely produced from early in
the season. The growth is
bushy but lax and arches over
as the plant begins to flower;
the foliage is pale green. In
common with other white
cultivars, 'Evensong' is prone
to botrytis, particularly in the
winter months.

DOREEN STROUD
Stroud, UK, 1988
Large, double flowers
(opposite). The tube and
sepals are red and the well-
formed, very full corolla is
lavender-blue. The growth is
vigorous but lax and trails
when the plant comes into
flower. An extremely free-
flowering cultivar suitable for
a hanging basket or standard.

FUCHSIA MAGELLANICA
V. MACROSTEMMA
'VERSICOLOR'
A variant of the species
Fuchsia magellanica. A small,
single flower (left) with red
tube and sepals and purple
corolla. The flowers are freely
produced on strong, upright,
arching growth. The foliage is
most attractively variegated
in cream, grey, and pink. An
extremely hardy variety
suitable for hedges, it is also a
great favourite with flower
arrangers. Listed by most
nurseries as 'Tricolor' or
'Tricolorii'.

CLIFTON BELLE
Handley, UK, 1974
Double (above). The long tube
and sepals are white and the
underside of the sepals is
tinged with pale pink. The
corolla is bright magenta. The
medium-sized blooms are
freely produced on upright
bushy growth.

LINDA GOULDING
Goulding, UK, 1981
Medium-sized, single flowers
(above). The tube and sepals
are very pale pink and the
corolla is white with pale pink
veining. The blooms are freely
produced on upright, bushy
growth. A good show plant
that will make a delightful
bush, standard, or pillar.

DARK EYES
Erickson, USA, 1958
A beautifully formed double flower (right). The tube and sepals are bright red and the very tight, full corolla is a deep violet-blue with red veining at the base of the outer petals. The blooms are very freely produced on bushy, upright growth. This cultivar makes a beautiful standard or bush. Awarded the American Fuchsia Society Certificate of Merit (1961).

BELVOIR BEAUTY
Gadsby, UK, 1975
Semi-double (opposite below). The buds of this cultivar are rounded and white and most attractive. The white tube and sepals open to reveal a pale blue corolla that is flushed with white at the base of the petals. The medium-sized pastel flowers are borne profusely on upright, bushy growth with light green foliage.

PHYLLIS
Introduced by Brown, UK, 1938
Small to medium-sized flowers (right) that are semi-double. The tube and sepals are rose-red and the corolla a deeper shade of the same colour. The habit is upright and bushy. 'Phyllis' can be trained to make a large standard, pillar, or pyramid.

CONSTANCE
Berkely Hort. Nursery, USA, 1935
Small, double flowers. The tube and sepals are pale pink and the corolla a deep blue-purple fading to purple. The growth is upright and quite bushy; the foliage is dark green. Synonymous with the plant sold as 'Heathfield' and very similar to the cultivar 'James Lye'.

BLUE WAVES
Waltz, USA, 1954
Large, double blooms. The tube and sepals are deep cerise. The corolla is a deep violet-blue, heavily streaked with cerise on the outer petals. The growth is upright and bushy and this cultivar makes a lovely standard. Awarded a Certificate of Merit in 1968 by the American Fuchsia Society.

MARY LOCKYER
Colville, UK, 1967
Large, double blooms. The tube and sepals are red and the corolla lavender and red. The inner petals are pale lavender veined with red and the outer petals are predominantly red but edged with lavender. As the flower matures the red of the corolla fades to pink. The growth is upright and vigorous and this cultivar will make a large specimen plant.

MISS CALIFORNIA
Hodges, USA, 1950
Semi-double. The tube and long sepals are pink. The long corolla is white with a faint tinge of pink and the petals are lightly veined with pink at the base. The medium-sized flowers are very freely produced on lax, slender stems. The growth is very bushy and compact, but this is not a vigorous cultivar.

PESTS, DISEASES, AND DISORDERS

Fuchsias are robust plants and not prone to disease or attack by many pests. Those growing in the open may suffer occasional damage from capsid bugs or caterpillars, but the more troublesome pests and diseases usually attack only those grown in the greenhouse. This is because pot-grown plants are entirely dependent on the grower to attend to their nutrition, watering, humidity, temperature, and general state of cleanliness. A well-grown plant is much less susceptible to pests and disease than one that has been starved and neglected.

Greenhouse hygiene is essential if plants are to be kept free from disease. In late summer, when the plants can be stood outside, the greenhouse and staging should be washed down and sterilized with a suitable disinfectant. Weeds should be removed from under the benches whenever they appear and fallen leaves and flowers should be constantly cleared away. Regular checks for signs of pests and diseases should be made and any minor problems treated promptly, as it is much more difficult to treat an established outbreak.

Insecticides and fungicides are available in a wide range of formulations either individually or sometimes as a mixture to provide a wide range of protection. They can be applied as wet sprays or, in the greenhouse, by igniting a special smoke cone that resembles a small firework. Smokes are very efficient and reach every crevice in the greenhouse but are more expensive than ordinary sprays. Fumigation should be done in the evening as the house must be completely closed down. The smoke must be allowed to work overnight and the following morning the greenhouse should be well ventilated.

Some preparations are harmful to certain plants and the instructions on the package should be studied to ensure that they are safe for use on fuchsias. Chemicals should be applied only in the evening or on dull days, as their use in sunlight can damage plants. When the plants are in flower smoke cones are less damaging to open blooms than wet sprays. Chemicals are available in two types, one kills on contact and the other is absorbed into the plant and transmitted via the sap to all parts. These latter formulations are called 'systemics' and are usually more effective and long lasting.

Some growers do not like using chemical insecticides and it is possible to buy biological controls that work by using natural predators or parasites against the pest. These may be purchased from specialists whose names can be obtained from gardening magazines or horticultural societies.

Pests

Aphids (greenfly, blackfly)   Aphids are the most common insects to attack fuchsias. These usually wingless, lice-like creatures suck the sap of the plant and are easily killed by the use of a systemic insecticide. Aphids are usually to be found on the soft growing tips of the plant, although their white discarded skins lying on the soil and leaves may first attract the gardener's attention. Their sap-sucking may cause distortion in the plant's growth and their honeydew secretions can cause a black mould to form. This mould will wash away if the plant is stood out in the rain. Systemic insecticides such as those containing dimethoate are most effective and give protection for up to three weeks. Partially systemic or non-systemic insecticides such as diazinon, gamma-HCH, or malathion must be used more frequently. Regular spraying is necessary because of the prolific breeding capabilities of the aphids.

Capsid bugs   These are bright, yellow-green insects that look rather like overgrown aphids. They are extremely active and spread rapidly. The insects suck the sap of the plant causing a variety of symptoms including distorted growth, holes in the leaves, and sometimes blindness in the growing tip (that is, the plant no longer grows from that point). Any of the systemic insecticides mentioned for aphids are also suitable for controlling capsid bugs.

Caterpillars   Some species of moth will occasionally lay eggs on garden fuchsias and the emerging caterpillars will eat holes in the leaves. They can be controlled by spraying with any suitable insecticide.

Greenhouse whitefly   This is without doubt the most troublesome pest to affect the fuchsia. The adults resemble tiny white moths and the eggs are invisible to the human eye. The juvenile stage appears as little white scales on the underside of the leaf. These scales are impervious to insecticides. It is necessary, therefore, to attack the adults as they emerge and before they have time to breed. Spray at ten-day intervals. The adults become immune to insecticides that are used on a regular basis and several different chemical types used in rotation are more effective. Permethrin, malathion, and gamma-HCH may be used in this rotation.

An infestation of whitefly may cause black mould on the plant; this should be washed away as recommended in the section on aphids (above).

Mealy bugs   There are two types of mealy bug, one that attacks the roots of plants and the other visible on the foliage and stems. The plant mealy bug reveals itself by the white tufts of waxy wool that cover its colonies. The bugs are small, pinky-white, segmented insects with a waxy surface which repels water, making them difficult to treat. They should be sprayed with an insecticide containing diazinon or malathion with a solvent to dissolve the waxy covering and allow the poison to penetrate. Root mealy bugs are usually spotted when potting-on; they leave blue-white deposits on the root ball and the plant pot. They can be controlled by immersing the root ball in a solution of malathion for several minutes, draining, and potting-on in the usual manner.

Red spider mites   This pest usually attacks only plants growing in unsuitable conditions. Fuchsias like a humid atmosphere and the red spider mite flourishes under hot dry conditions. The mite is barely visible to the naked eye and the first sign of an infestation is a brown mottling on the underside of the leaves. In severe cases the leaves become crisp and eventually fall and they may be covered with a fine silk web. Very few of the insecticides available to the amateur are effective against this pest and probably the best treatment is to prune back any affected plants and remove all remaining leaves. The plant can be repotted to encourage fresh young growth. Fumigating the house with an azobenzene smoke should clear any remaining mites but as they spread rapidly all the plants should be rechecked periodically. To lessen the chances of a recurrence, shade the greenhouse to reduce the temperature, dampen the paths to increase humidity, and mist the foliage with clean rain water.

Sciarid flies   These are small black flies that lay their eggs in the compost. Their emerging larvae will eat the young roots of cuttings or seedlings but rarely damage mature plants. Watering the affected compost with a solution of malathion or stirring some gamma-HCH powder into the top layer of compost will eliminate this pest. Sciarid flies are most commonly found in soilless composts that have been overwatered.

Vine weevils   Adult vine weevils thrive in plant debris, so this should be removed regularly from the greenhouse floor and staging to keep the pest at bay. The adult does not harm fuchsias, but its larvae eat the roots, making the plants unexpectedly wilt. When repotting, the caterpillar-like grubs can be seen in the soil. Stirring gamma-HCH powder into the surface of the compost is the most effective treatment, but vine weevils are difficult to eradicate and successive treatments may be necessary.

Other insect pests, such as thrips and leafhoppers, may occur from time to time but are effectively controlled by the regular use of insecticides.

Diseases

Fuchsia rust   This disease can affect fuchsias both in the greenhouse and in the garden. It is a fungal infection and is spread by tiny spores that are carried by the wind. The disease is typified by eruptions of rust-coloured powdery rings, usually on the underside of the leaves but in a severe attack also on the upper surfaces of the leaves and on the stems. Rust is difficult to control because the fungus grows inside the plant tissue, not on the surface. Infected plant material should be removed and burned. To kill the spores, the plants should then be sprayed with a fungicide containing mancozeb, maneb, thiram, or zineb plus a wetting agent. Spraying should be repeated as directed in the manufacturer's instructions until the plant is clear of the disease.

Botrytis cineria   This is a fungal parasite, commonly known as grey mould, which affects leaves, stems, and dormant growth buds. It thrives in cold, stagnant air. All infected material should be removed and burnt and the plant sprayed with a fungicide containing benomyl or thiram. Alternating the use of different fungicides gives the most effective control of botrytis, because resistant strains readily occur. The risk of attack can be minimized by keeping the plants and greenhouse free of fallen leaves and flowers and ventilating whenever possible. Heating the air (electrically) will dry the atmosphere and will also help to keep the disease in check.

Disorders

Leaf discoloration and fall   Leaves may discolour for several reasons. Moving a plant outside, away from the protection of the greenhouse, without sufficient hardening off, will cause the foliage to become purple. The plants will outgrow this, but they will have suffered a severe check and flowering will be delayed.

During the summer months, plants grown under glass sometimes develop a red or purple tinge to their leaves. This is usually a sign of nitrogen deficiency and the feed should be changed to one with a higher nitrogen content.

In the autumn the leaves will naturally become discoloured before they fall, but a certain number of the lower leaves may fall at any time of the year. If the leaves look dull and begin to fall before the autumn, the plant should be checked for red spider mites.

Root loss   The most common reasons for a plant to lose its roots are overwatering and overfeeding. The remedies are outlined in the section on cultivation (pages 19 and 21).

FUCHSIAS IN THE HOUSE AND GARDEN

Fuchsias in the house

Greenhouse-raised fuchsias should not be moved into the house when they are on the point of flowering; the dry atmosphere indoors will often cause the buds to drop within forty-eight hours, followed soon after by the leaves.

Usually the most vigorous plants such as the hardy cultivars are recommended for growing indoors because they are better fitted to withstand the adverse environment. However, any fuchsias that have been grown indoors from the early stages will, to a large extent, have adapted to the environment and be more successful as house plants. The best room in the house for growing fuchsias is the kitchen, where the atmosphere is relatively moist (bathrooms are often too dark). The best position is on a windowsill facing east or west. A north-facing window ledge will probably not receive sufficient light, while a south-facing position will be too hot and dry. Plants grown indoors should be potted-on, watered, and fed as described for greenhouse plants.

A close watch must be kept on the plants as an infestation of red spider mite (see page 115) is much more likely indoors. A daily spray with clean rain water will act as a deterrent, but remove any affected fuchsias immediately, as the infestation will spread rapidly to any other plants.

Fuchsias will also make good decorative features in a well-ventilated conservatory, although a south-facing one will probably need some shading in the height of summer.

Fuchsias as half-hardy garden plants

All the forms of trained fuchsias can be used as decorative features in the garden but the most usual are hanging baskets, standards, and bush-trained forms.

Standards are used to provide height in formal bedding schemes or in patio tubs. Unfortunately they are particularly susceptible to wind damage, so it is advisable to choose a sheltered position and stake the plant firmly so that it cannot be blown over. Ties must secure the head to the stake or it can snap off completely in a strong wind. The main branches of the head must also be supported.

Standards can be underplanted with bush fuchsias or any of the usual summer bedding plants. The Victorians were very fond of bright clashing colours and would plant marigolds and lobelia under deep red and purple fuchsias. The marigolds may well have had a beneficial effect as they attract hover flies, the larvae of which eat greenfly. Standards in large decorative pots can also be underplanted with trailing fuchsias which cascade down over the sides of the container. Busy lizzies (*Impatiens*) are shade-loving plants that come in many colours and the modern compact cultivars are ideal for underplanting standard fuchsias. However, as fuchsias have rather shallow roots, care should be taken when planting or weeding.

Bush fuchsias are very useful and can be used to fill any bare patches in the flower border. There are suitable fuchsias for almost any position in the garden, some make ground-cover plants, others can be used on the rockery. Some grow tall and upright, others are spreading or compact – the variations in growth and flower are endless.

Fuchsias in baskets (see pages 29–30) can be mixed with other subjects for added variety. The grey-leaved *Cineraria maritima*, decorative-leaved ivies, and tradescantias will all provide interesting foliage that contrasts beautifully with the fuchsia flowers. *Campanula isophylla*, *Begonia semperflorens*, and *Impatiens* are also good companion plants. Avoid, though, trailing lobelias and petunias, which grow so rampantly that they overwhelm the fuchsias.

Provided that they are fed and cared for properly, fuchsias have a very long flowering season and are therefore ideal subjects for patio decoration and summer bedding.

Fuchsias for permanent garden planting

The term 'hardy fuchsia' applies to those cultivars that when planted out of doors will survive despite being killed back to ground level by the frost and snow. In very hard winters or in exceptionally harsh climates, though, even the hardiest may succumb. In places where the temperature rarely falls below freezing, most cultivars will prove hardy and it is in these areas that some fuchsias can assume tree-like proportions.

Fuchsias will grow in almost any type of well-cultivated soil although they prefer a slightly acid one. Chalky soils may prove a little too well drained for fuchsias in summer but, to some extent, this can be rectified by mulching and watering during prolonged dry spells. Poorly drained areas that remain very wet for considerable periods are unlikely to be suitable areas for growing fuchsias.

Hardy fuchsias that have been raised in the greenhouse should not be planted out until they are filling a 4–5in (10–13cm) pot. Larger plants than this are less suitable as they take longer to establish in the garden and are more likely to die in the first winter. The plants should be hardened off and when there is no

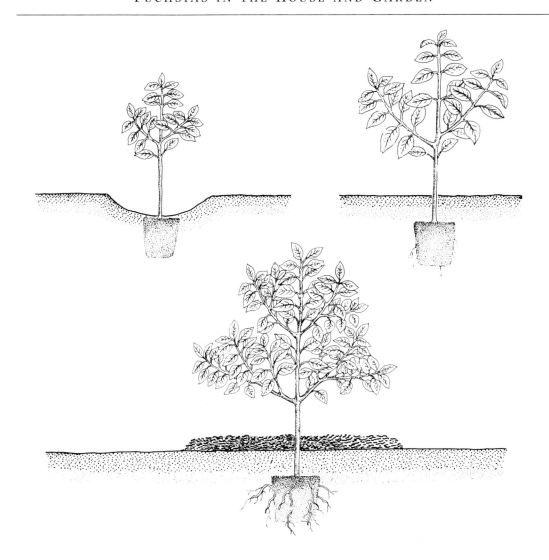

longer any danger of frost they can be planted out. All planting should be done between the end of May and the first half of July or the plants will not have sufficient time to establish before the first winter.

Hardy fuchsias are most likely to survive the winter in an open sunny position where their stems can ripen properly before the onset of severe weather.

To provide protection from the cold it is essential to plant fuchsias quite deeply so that the bottom part of the main stem is about 4in (10cm) below soil level. To prevent a sudden check, this should be accomplished by planting in a slight depression and gradually filling it in with soil as the plant grows (see diagram above). After a hard winter, fresh growth will be made from this underground stem. It is beneficial, when planting, to work a small handful of blood, fish, and bone fertilizer into the soil around the roots. The bone meal, being rich in phosphates, will promote root growth and the blood and fish will gradually decompose releasing other nutrients required by the growing plant. Organic fertilizers are less likely than chemical fertilizers to scorch the roots of young plants, because their nutrients are not immediately released.

Plants that have been grown in a soilless compost will establish more readily in the garden if a little peat is mixed in with the soil at planting time. Fuchsias should be watered in after planting and care should be taken to ensure that they do not dry out until well established. In a period of drought even mature plants may wilt and watering will be necessary.

When autumn comes the plants should not be pruned; the old wood, if allowed to remain, will continue to offer some protection to the crown. To protect the plants in their first winter it is advisable to spread a layer of peat 2–4in (5–10cm) deep around the plant for extra insulation. This can also give added protection to established plants in subsequent winters.

In the following spring most plants should be showing new growth. Any dead wood should then be removed completely and in mild areas it may be necessary to prune live stems back a little to prevent the plants becoming overlarge and woody round the base. A handful of organic fertilizer worked into the soil around the base of the plant will encourage healthy new growth and promote early flowering.

The variegated or golden-foliaged hardy fuchsias look decorative long before they flower and this can be an added attraction, particularly in a small garden.

Some of the more vigorous hardy fuchsias can be used not only as specimen bushes but also as hedges to divide one area of the garden from another. The position of the hedge will influence the choice of cultivar. For example, near to a path, a strong, upright-growing plant like 'Prosperity' (see page 33) would be more suitable than the spreading *F. magellanica* (see pages 106–7). Hedges of a mixture of cultivars are unsatisfactory because they grow unevenly and generally look untidy. An exception to this is a hedge comprised of differently coloured sports from the same parent – for example, 'Lady Thumb', 'Tom Thumb', and 'Son of Thumb'. The 'Thumbs' are all very compact dwarf plants and are very suitable as a dividing hedge in a small garden. Sports with variegated foliage are always less vigorous than their green-leaved counterparts and are unsuitable for mixed planting.

The number of plants required for a given length of hedge will depend upon the particular cultivar chosen. The upright-growing types will need to be planted at intervals of 18in (45cm) against 24in (60cm) for the large, spreading ones.

When planting a hedge, a trench of about a spade's depth is dug and some well-rotted manure mixed with the subsoil. The trench is partially filled in and the plants are then planted at appropriate intervals in the manner described above for individual specimens. Any surplus soil can be spread away from the edges of the trench but gradually returned as the plants become established.

Pruning the hedge should take place in the spring and be confined to the removal of dead wood and any untidy stems. A top dressing of well-rotted manure or peat each autumn will keep the soil in good condition and an application of fertilizer in the spring will provide the nutrients for continued healthy growth.

Overwintering non-hardy fuchsias

There are several ways of overwintering non-hardy fuchsias and the method chosen will depend largely on whether a greenhouse or conservatory is available and how much the grower is prepared to spend on heating it.

The ideal, but expensive, way is to keep the plants in a greenhouse heated to a minimum temperature of 44–50°F (7–10°C). These cosseted plants will continue to grow very slowly and will come into flower much earlier than those that are rested completely. In the autumn, pot-grown fuchsias should be trimmed back by removing approximately two-thirds of each stem using sharp secateurs. This pruning should be carried out bearing in mind the overall shape of the plant. Plants brought in from the garden should be pruned in a similar manner. The soil should be carefully shaken from the roots and the plants potted individually into the smallest container that will just accommodate the root system; extra long roots may be pruned if necessary. The plants should be placed on the greenhouse staging (preferably slatted) with as much space around them as possible to encourage free circulation of air. Any dead or yellow leaves should be removed regularly and the plants sprayed with fungicide to prevent mould and botrytis.

Most greenhouse growers will maintain a temperature of only 32–41°F (0–5°C), which is too low for growth to occur. The plants must be 'rested' (kept in a dormant state by withholding water) until the leaves fall; but plants should not be allowed to become dust-dry or they will die. Some cultivars that produce a lot of woody growth, such as 'Celia Smedley', can be placed on their sides under the bench, as this seems to encourage shooting from the base in the spring. At this temperature young plants cannot be overwintered successfully and are best taken indoors and grown on the windowsill.

The two most common causes of losses during the winter are plant roots being allowed to dry out completely and failure to keep a minimum temperature of at least 32°F (0°C) on the coldest nights. The easiest way to check that the minimum temperature does not fall below freezing point, even during the middle of the night, is to invest in a maximum/minimum thermometer.

When plants begin to show signs of life in the early spring, they benefit greatly from being repotted. They should be removed from their pots, the old soil and any dead roots carefully shaken away, and repotted, with fresh compost, into, preferably, a smaller pot.

Watering should be gradually increased as the days become warmer and growth accelerates. The plants should be fed or potted on as necessary and most cultivars will start to flower in June.

It is also possible to overwinter fuchsias in an unheated greenhouse or garden frame by providing the roots and the lower part of the stems with sufficient insulation to keep out the frost. The plants are left in the garden or cold greenhouse as long as possible – a slight frost will not kill them. They are then removed from their pots or dug up from the garden and excess compost shaken from the roots. The stems are trimmed back by two-thirds and any remaining leaves removed. The fuchsias are then replanted close together in the greenhouse border and covered with a layer of peat at least 6in (15cm) deep. A variation of this method is to bury the plants on their sides in a hole about 12in (30cm) deep dug in the greenhouse border. The replaced soil effectively insulates them from the cold and frost. Alternatively, if the greenhouse has no border, they may be placed in an insulating layer of peat in a large box, keeping a distance of at least 6–9in (15–23cm) between the plants and sides of the box. If the box is stood on the floor rather than on a bench the surface area through which the frost can penetrate is reduced. It is essential not to let the plants dry out completely and, if necessary, the insulating peat or soil should be lightly dampened.

The plants are unearthed in early March or when the worst of the winter is past, repotted into fresh compost, and stood in the cold greenhouse or frame. On any subsequent frosty nights the plants can be protected with layers of newspaper, but these must be removed in the daytime. Water sparingly at first until the plants start to grow rapidly.

For those growers who do not have the luxury of a greenhouse or garden frame, it is possible to overwinter non-hardy fuchsias in the open garden. A trench should be dug in a sheltered position, of sufficient depth to take the fuchsias with at least 6in (15cm) between the top of the root ball and the surface of the soil. If it is necessary, the stems of large plants should be pruned accordingly. The bottom of the trench should be lined with broken crocks or straw or anything that will provide good drainage. The sides should be lined with polythene to prevent excessive ingress of water. The plants are then stood along the trench and peat is poured in around them until the trench is filled. A layer of polythene is then laid over the surface to keep off the worst of the rain and held in position by some of the excavated soil. The fuchsias should be unearthed in late March, repotted, and stood in the open trench on slates or upturned saucers to prevent worms infesting the compost. Cover the plants at night with cloches or newspaper and polythene to keep off late spring frosts. They should also be covered on wet days to prevent them becoming waterlogged. As the plants grow and need more room they can be stood out in the shelter of the house until they can be planted in the open garden or patio tubs.

A SELECTION OF CULTIVARS

Alice Hoffman

Klese, Germany, 1911

Semi-double. The tube and sepals are deep rose and the corolla is creamy white with veining of deep rose. The flowers are small but borne in profusion. The growth is upright, bushy, and compact. The foliage is a most attractive bronze colour, particularly when grown in full light. Hardy.

Annabel

Ryle, UK, 1977

Double. The tube and sepals are white, slightly flushed with pink, and the full corolla is white with a slight pink veining. The pink tinge becomes more pronounced if the plant is grown in full light or lacks nitrogen. The tube is quite long and the broad sepals that recurve at the tips are held well out from the tube. The growth is upright but arches gracefully under the weight of the fairly large blooms, which are very freely produced. The foliage is a greenish yellow and the veining in the leaf is quite pronounced. The habit is good with short-jointed, compact growth. 'Annabel' makes an excellent show plant.

Applause

Stubbs, USA, 1978

Double. The short, thick tube and broad sepals are pink, although the sepals have a white mid-stripe. The full, open corolla is salmon-orange that deepens in colour as the flower ages. The flowers are large and freely produced. The growth is extremely vigorous although lax in habit and this cultivar makes a superb hanging basket.

The leaves are mid-green, broad, and large. Mrs Annabelle Stubbs, who raised 'Applause', also introduced the lovely cultivars 'Nancy Lou' (see page 76), 'Pink Marshmallow', and 'Dancing Flame'.

Army Nurse

Hodges, USA, 1947

Semi-double. The short, slightly bulbous tube and sepals are deep red and the corolla violet-blue with a pink flush at the base of the petals. The flowers are small but very freely produced and show good resistance to bad weather. The growth is strong, sturdy, and upright. 'Army Nurse' makes a lovely subject for the shrub border. Pacific Grove in California has this fuchsia as its official flower, thanks to the efforts of two residents – its raiser, Raymond Hodges, and his wife Merle. Hardy.

Auntie Jinks

Wilson, UK, 1970

Single. The tube is deep pink and the sepals white with a deep pink edge. The corolla is purple with a white flush. The flowers are small but abundant and extremely attractive. The leaves are small and mid-green. The habit is pendulous but very compact and ideal for basket work. The petite growth also makes it suitable for a table standard. This was a chance seedling from 'Checkerboard', to which it bears little resemblance.

Barbara

Tolley, UK, 1971

Single. The short tube and upturning

sepals are pale pink and the semi-flared corolla is salmon pink. The growth is upright, very vigorous, and inclined to spread. It is necessary constantly to pinch this cultivar to produce a good bush; with training it makes a lovely standard. The medium-sized blooms fall quite soon after opening but, because the flowers are borne in profusion and the plant is self-cleaning (that is, it drops the fruits at the same time as the flowers), this is not a drawback. The strong growth also makes it an ideal plant for summer bedding and it does well in a sunny position.

Beacon
Bull, UK, 1871
Single. The tube and sepals are deep pink and the corolla is mauvish-pink. The medium-sized flowers are freely produced and show well against the dark green foliage. The growth is upright, compact, and bushy and this old cultivar makes a good show plant in any form. It was awarded a Highly Commended Certificate in the British Royal Horticultural Society's trial of hardy fuchsias at Wisley (1975–8).

Beacon Rosa
Bürgi-Ott, Switzerland, 1972
Single. The tube and sepals are deep pink and the corolla a beautiful rose pink and most attractive. The foliage, growth, and flower shape are almost identical with 'Beacon', from which this is almost certainly a sport. Recent trials would suggest that it is also as hardy as 'Beacon'.

Belsay Beauty
Ryle, UK, 1975
Semi-double. The tube and sepals are pink but the upper surface of the sepals is flushed with white. The corolla is violet-blue aging to deep mauve, and the variation in colour between the young and old flowers is quite attractive. The buds are short and rounded and the medium-sized flowers are freely produced. When in flower the branches arch gracefully and this cultivar can be used effectively in a

hanging basket. The pale to mid-green foliage is borne on compact, upright growth. 'Belsay Beauty' makes a good specimen bush or standard. It was awarded the British Fuchsia Society's Certificate of Merit in 1975.

Bishop's Bells
Gadsby, UK, 1970
Semi-double. The tube and sepals are deep pink-red and the sepals are very long with green tips. The corolla is a deep violet fading to red-purple and the petals are veined with a deep pink-red. The bell-shaped flowers are large, sometimes up to 5in (12·5cm) across the open sepals. This is a strong, upright, vigorous plant with dark green foliage that makes a lovely large bush. It has a higher nitrogen requirement than some fuchsias.

Blue Bush
Gadsby, UK, 1973
Single. A small- to medium-sized flower with rosy red tube and sepals and a deep blue corolla veined with the rose-red. In the garden the habit is strong, upright, and bushy, but in the greenhouse the growth is more lax and arching. The leaves are quite small and dark green. This is a reliable hardy cultivar, suitable as a hedge.

Blue Elf
Hall, UK, 1968
Single. The tube and sepals are pink and the short, narrow sepals curl back with a sideways twist towards the tube. The bell-shaped corolla is light blue with violet edges, flushed with a paler blue at the base of the petals and veined in pink. The medium-sized flowers are very freely produced from early in the season. The growth is upright and bushy and the leaves mid-green with serrated edges. A lovely show plant, 'Blue Elf' won a British Fuchsia Society Award of Merit in 1972.

Blush o' Dawn
Martin, USA, 1962
Double. The tube and sepals are waxy white with green tips and the very full

corolla is a pale silver-blue. The plant unfortunately lacks vigour and requires careful cultivation but the delicate flower colour makes it worth persevering with. The mid-green foliage is carried on upright growth, but when the plant blooms the weight of the fairly large flowers causes the rather weak growth to trail. Two-year-old plants with a framework of mature wood make good bush plants. A cultivar that appreciates greenhouse protection or a shady, sheltered corner, 'Blush o' Dawn' was considered by its raiser, George Martin, to be his best introduction – better even than 'Sophisticated Lady' and 'Orange Drops' (see pages 63 and 102).

Bountiful
Munkner, USA, 1963

Double. The tube and sepals are pale pink, tipped with green. The corolla is very full and creamy white with pink veining at the base of the petals. The foliage is mid-green and borne on strong, upright, bushy growth. The weight of the large and freely produced flowers makes it necessary to support the branches well while the plant is in bloom. There is another single cultivar called 'Bountiful', raised by James Lye in Britain, a cross between 'Arabella Improved' and 'James Lye'. However, most nurseries in Britain which list 'Bountiful' seem to stock the United States double.

Buttercup
Paskesen, USA, 1976

Single. The short tube and sepals are flesh pink and the underside of the sepals tinted with orange. The sepals stand away from the corolla but curve towards it at the tips. The flaring corolla has four petals and is a clear, bright orange – not, unfortunately, the yellow that the name suggests. The growth is upright and bushy with mid-green leaves. The medium-sized flowers produce their best colour when the plant is grown in the shade. Mr Paskesen was a keen hybridist who worked with a view to raising the first double orange fuchsia and came very close with 'Bicentennial' (see page 94) in 1976.

Cascade
Lagen, USA, 1937

Single. The tube and long, slender sepals are white flushed with cherry-red and the corolla is a deep cherry-red. The growth is cascading as the name suggests but fairly compact and this cultivar makes an excellent hanging basket. Although the medium-sized flowers are produced only on the trailing stems, the attractive mid-green foliage of this useful fuchsia covers the basket well.

Celia Smedley
Roe, UK, 1970

Single. The tube and sepals are pale pink and the corolla a bright currant red. The flowers are quite large and the contrast in colour between the sepals and corolla is striking. The habit is upright, bushy, and extremely vigorous. The young stems are greenish white, but this cultivar produces a lot of wood even in its first year and makes a rather unattractive plant in its second year unless induced to shoot from the base. The leaves are mid-green with serrated edges. This strong-growing plant makes a good subject for a patio tub, although bright sunlight deepens the colour of the sepals and the contrast between corolla and sepals is then less pronounced. A seedling from 'Joy Patmore' and 'Glitters'.

Charming
Lye, UK, 1895

Single. The tube and sepals are deep red and the corolla bright purple fading to red-purple. The growth is upright and bushy but arches gracefully under the weight of the medium-sized blooms. The foliage of a young cutting is pale green but, as the plant grows, this becomes a delightful yellow-green which is maintained throughout the season. The colour of the foliage is responsible for this cultivar often being confused with 'Drame' raised by Lemoine in France (1880), although the flowers of 'Drame' are usually semi-double. 'Charming' makes an attractive plant for the garden. Hardy.

Checkerboard
Walker and Jones, USA, 1948
Single. The long tube is red and the sepals are white but flushed with red where they join the tube. The corolla is a deep, bright red. The medium-sized flowers, long and elegant in shape, are produced in profusion. The growth is upright and vigorous and the leaves mid-green. One of the best cultivars for exhibition work as it is easily trained. This cultivar makes a spectacular large standard and although the branches are at first stiff and upright, they arch gracefully under the mass of bloom.

Chillerton Beauty
Bass, UK, 1847
Single. The tube and sepals are pale pink, tipped with green, and the corolla is blue-violet veined with pink. The small flowers are freely produced on strong, upright growth. The leaves are dark green. 'Chillerton Beauty' makes a good, low hedge. It is identical with cultivars sold as 'Query' and 'General Tom Thumb'. Hardy.

Cliff's Hardy
Gadsby, UK, 1966
Single. Tube and sepals are deep pink-red, tipped with green, and the corolla blue-violet veined with red. The medium-sized flowers are freely produced and held erect, a trait inherited from one of its parents 'Bon Accorde' (see page 77). The growth is upright and bushy. 'Cliff's Hardy' makes an attractive garden plant with the flowers clearly visible. Hardy.

Cliff's Unique
Gadsby, UK, 1976
Double. The short, thick tube is pale pink and the green-tipped sepals are initially waxy-white flushed with pink but mature to all pink. The full corolla is a pale violet-blue and very attractive. The medium-sized blooms are very freely produced and held out well from the plant and, when bedded in the garden, the flowers are often held erect. The foliage is blue-green and the habit compact and upright. This cultivar makes a fine bush or standard.

Clifton Charm
Handley, UK, 1981
Single. The short tube is cerise and the thick sepals reflexing back to the tube are a bright cerise. The corolla is deep lilac flushed with pink at the base of the petals that are edged and veined in cerise. The medium-sized flowers are bell shaped and have a long pistil and red stamens. The growth is upright and bushy and the short-jointed stems are red. The foliage is mid- to dark green and serrated at the edges. This cultivar has a proven record of hardiness and planting it in full sun accentuates the colours of the flowers.

Cloverdale Pearl
Gadsby, UK, 1974
Single. The tube and sepals are pink with a white flush and tipped with green. The tips of the sepals curve back towards the tube revealing the creamy-white corolla. The dark green, shiny foliage is produced on upright, bushy growth and contrasts well with the pale blooms. The medium-sized flowers are freely produced. 'Cloverdale Pearl' is an ideal show plant, whether trained as a large bush, standard, or pillar.

Constellation
Schnabel, USA, 1957
Double. The tube and sepals are white, tipped with green. The corolla is creamy white. The leaves are dark green and serrated at the edges. The growth is moderately upright but the stems arch gracefully under the weight of bloom produced. The fairly large flowers are beautifully formed and this cultivar is one of the purest whites available. Cuttings of 'Constellation' root spasmodically and generally take longer than most other cultivars. A two-year-old plant with a good framework of woody growth makes a lovely bush plant and this cultivar also makes a beautiful standard.

Coquet Bell
Ryle-Atkinson, UK, 1973
Single. The tube and sepals are deep rose pink and the corolla pale mauve, flushed with pink at the base of the petals and

veined with red. The sepals recurve, revealing the bell-shaped corolla. The flowers are freely produced and held out well from the foliage. The growth is upright and short-jointed and easily trained as a specimen bush. This cultivar also makes a delightful standard.

Coquet Dale
Ryle, UK, 1976
Double. The short tube and short, wide sepals are pink and the sepals recurve until they almost touch the tube. The corolla is pale lilac-blue. The growth is strong, bushy, and upright and the leaves midgreen. 'Coquet Dale' is easy to train as a show plant and it also makes a fine decorative plant in a patio tub. However, the medium-sized flowers are a more delicate colour if the plant is grown in the shade. This is a seedling from 'Joe Kusber' and 'Northumbrian Belle' (see page 133).

Corallina
Prince, UK, 1844
Single. The tube and sepals are a bright scarlet and the corolla a deep purple that fades to a red-purple. The sepals do not reflex at all and the flowers are medium in size. The growth is vigorous and arching. The foliage and stems are dark green but have a deep red tone that makes this a most attractive garden plant. 'Corallina' is a reliably hardy cultivar. It makes an excellent cut flower and the mature foliage stands well in water, so this is a valuable plant for the flower arranger. There is also a variegated form, 'Corallina Variegata', raised by the Institut Horticole at Liège in Belgium.

Cottinghamii
Raiser unknown
Single. The tube and sepals are bright red and the petals orange-red. The flowers are tiny, measuring only about $\frac{3}{8}$in (9mm) across from sepal tip to sepal tip. The flowers are succeeded by glossy brown-purple fruits that look like little beads. The foliage is also small, dainty, and dark green in colour. The growth is slow and upright in the garden but much more vigorous and lax under glass. This cultivar is hardy in a sheltered position in the garden. 'Cottinghamii' belongs to the Breviflorae group of cultivars but the flowers are slightly larger and more showy than those of most members of this group.

Crackerjack
Walker, USA, 1961
Single or semi-double. The tube and long sepals are white, flushed with pale pink that deepens in colour as the flowers age. The corolla is pale blue with a white flush at the base of the petals and lightly veined with pink. The corolla matures to a pale mauve. The large flowers have long petals and are rather loosely formed. The habit is vigorous and cascading, making this an ideal subject for a large hanging basket.

Cream Puff
Kennett, USA, 1960
Double. The long, slender tube is pale pink and the gently recurving sepals are pink at the base but shade to white at the tips. The corolla is a creamy white with a delicate pink flush on the outer petals. The blooms are quite large and frilled. The foliage is dark green and the growth compact and lax. This cultivar can sometimes be difficult to root but subsequently grows well. 'Cream Puff' will make a pretty hanging basket or half standard. It is similar to the cultivar 'So Big'.

Curly Q
Kennett, USA, 1961
Single. The tube is white flushed with carmine and the sepals are pale carmine. The sepals reflex back in a circular manner to touch the tube and it is this feature that suggested its name. The corolla is violet-blue and the petals folded. The rather small foliage is grey-green and the stems deep red-green. The growth is quite lax but is suitable for training into most forms. Being a floriferous and unusual cultivar it makes an appealing show plant. Awarded the American Fuchsia Society's Certificate of Merit (1964).

Daisy Bell
Registered by Miescke, USA, 1977
Single flower similar in shape to the Triphylla hybrids. The long tube is pink overlaid with orange. The sepals are pale pink-orange at the base becoming a greenish white towards the tips; they are less than $\frac{1}{2}$in (1cm) long and held almost at right angles to the tube. The small corolla is salmon-pink and the four petals make a cone less than $\frac{1}{2}$in (1cm). The flowers are freely produced but not until rather late in the season. The foliage is a lightly bronzed green and the habit is compact, lax, and suitable for hanging baskets.

Dancing Flame
Stubbs, USA, 1981
Double. The short, thick tube is pale orange-pink and the wide, flared sepals a slightly deeper shade. The corolla is orange and carmine. The petals are mainly deep orange with streaks of carmine at the edges. The first blooms may only be semi-double but the later ones are fully double. The stems are very pale green, almost white, and the serrated-edged leaves are dark green. The growth is arching rather than lax. This is a reliable early-flowering cultivar suitable for the showbench.

Derby Imp
Gadsby, UK, 1974
Single. The slender tube and sepals are crimson and the corolla violet-blue, deepening in colour as the flower matures. The small, dainty flowers are produced in profusion from early in the season. The foliage is also small and dark green in colour. The growth is vigorous and lax, making this an excellent cultivar for basket work. Regular pinching in the early stages of growth is essential as the plant produces long, sweeping trails if left unchecked. Unfortunately red/violet-blue flowers are unfashionable today and this cultivar is less popular than it deserves to be.

Empress of Prussia
Hoppe, UK, 1868
Single. The tube and sepals are bright red and the corolla reddish-magenta. The flowers are quite large and freely produced, each pair of leaf axils bearing six to eight flowers instead of the usual two. The growth is vigorous and upright and the foliage dark green and shiny. 'Empress of Prussia' has proved extremely hardy in cultivation. It is almost identical to the cultivar 'Monsieur Thibaut' (see pages 97–9), the main difference being that approximately one in twenty of the flowers produced by 'Empress of Prussia' has five sepals instead of four. In Britain it is very difficult to obtain 'Empress of Prussia' as most of the nurseries listing this cultivar actually supply 'Monsieur Thibaut'.

Eternal Flame
Paskesen, USA, 1941
Semi-double. The tube and sepals are salmon pink, tipped with green and the corolla dusky rose splashed with orange, shading to pale salmon at the base of the petals. The medium-to-large flowers are freely produced throughout the season and in a heated greenhouse this cultivar will continue to bloom into the late autumn. The growth is strong, bushy, and upright, and the foliage is dark green. Excellent for summer bedding or patio tubs, it also makes a good show plant.

Expo 86
Wood, USA, 1986
Double. Pink tube and sepals white on the upper surface and pink-orange on the underside. The sepals fully recurve revealing the bright red and orange corolla. The colour of the flowers is most striking when the plant is grown in the shade. The growth is vigorous but trailing and this cultivar will make an excellent hanging basket.

Flash
Hazard and Hazard, USA, 1930
Single. A small, bright red flower, freely produced on strong upright growth. The foliage is also small and a shiny mid-green. 'Flash' is accepted by the British Fuchsia Society as show-bench hardy.

Flying Cloud
Reiter, USA, 1949

Double. The tube and sepals are white with a slight flush of pink that becomes much more pronounced if the plant is grown in full light. The sepals gradually recurve as the flower matures and the corolla is white and full. The growth is rather lax and spreading and the foliage dark green and serrated at the edge. When grown in the shade, this is one of the best double white cultivars but it is similar to 'Constellation', which is easier to propagate and grow.

Frau Hilde Rademacher
Rademacher, Germany, 1925

Double. The short bulbous tube and broad, recurving sepals are red and the beautiful, tightly packed corolla a deep lilac-blue that ages to purple. The formation of the corolla is reminiscent of 'Dark Eyes' (see page 109). The medium-sized flowers are freely produced on vigorous, upright growth that arches as the plant comes into bloom. It is considered to be a hardy fuchsia in most areas of Britain and makes a most attractive garden plant.

Garden News
Handley, UK, 1978

Double. The short, broad tube is pale pink and the sepals (which do not recurve) are also pink. The corolla is bright magenta with an overlay of orange at the base and around the edge of the petals. The large blooms are freely produced, usually four blooms at each pair of leaf axils. The growth is vigorous and upright but not very bushy. The leaves are wide, dark green, and serrated at the edges. This cultivar produces many three-leaved cuttings, invaluable for growing as standards. Grown under glass it will make a good exhibition plant but it has also proved to be hardy in most areas of Britain and the unusual colouring of the blooms makes it a welcome addition to the garden.

Gilda
Handley, UK, 1971

Double. The short tube and broad sepals are pale coral pink and the very full corolla deep rose with red edges to the petals. The growth is lax, trailing under the weight of the large flowers, so 'Gilda' makes a beautiful hanging basket. The foliage is yellowish-green with red veining and the broad leaves are lightly serrated. A particularly vigorous and free-flowering cultivar that makes a superb show plant.

Golden Anniversary
Stubbs, USA, 1980

Double. The thick tube is white tinged with green and the broad, sharply pointed sepals are white. The corolla is very dark purple, fading in colour with age. The base of each petal is flushed with pink. The new foliage is yellow-green maturing to a pale green. The growth is heavy, self-branching, and trailing in habit. An interesting colour combination for hanging baskets and standards.

Gruss aus dem Bodethal
Sattler and Belge, Germany, 1838

Single to semi-double. The tube and sepals are a deep red and the sepals are held out horizontally from the corolla, recurving for approximately half their length. The corolla is deep purple to almost black when the flower first opens and streaked with deep red at the base of the petals. The flowers are fairly small and profuse but unfortunately are produced rather late in the season. The growth is upright, bushy, and compact. When bedded in the garden the growth is even more restricted and it makes a dwarf bush. This cultivar is thought to be identical with 'Black Prince', introduced by Banks in Britain (1861).

Harry Gray
Dunnett, UK, 1980

Double. The tube is white, streaked heavily with pink, and the sepals are white and veined at the base with pink. The full corolla is white with only an occasional tinge of pink, although this becomes more pronounced in strong light. The flowers are medium-to-small in size and this is an exceptionally free-flowering cultivar. The growth is wiry, very bushy, and trailing; the leaves are small and dark green. This is an outstanding recent introduction that makes an excellent and reliable show plant. A versatile fuchsia, it is superb as a hanging basket, table standard, or half standard.

Heidi Weiss
Tacolneston Nurseries, UK, 1973
Double. The tube and sepals are crimson red and the corolla is white, veined with red. The growth is upright and bushy and the leaves dark green. The medium-sized flowers are freely produced from early in the season. This is a sport from 'Heidi Ann' (see page 79) and is identical with the sport 'White Ann' introduced by Wills-Atkinson in 1972. Like 'Heidi Ann', it has proved reliably hardy in most areas of Britain. An attractive garden plant and suitable for all show work.

Hula Girl
Paskesen, USA, 1972
Double. The tube and sepals are rose-red and the very full corolla is creamy white streaked with rose at the base of the petals. The flowers are very large and freely produced. The growth is extremely vigorous and lax, making this an ideal subject for a large hanging basket. The stems are red. One attraction of this fuchsia is the red veining in the dark green leaves, which shows most prominently when 'Hula Girl' is growing in full light.

Iced Champagne
Jennings, UK, 1968
Single. The tube and sepals are a soft pink and the long, pointed sepals recurve until they almost touch the tube. The long corolla is very pale pink. The flowers are medium in size and very freely produced. The growth is very bushy, compact, and short jointed. This is a beautiful seedling from 'Miss California' (which it resembles; see page 112), but its habit is very much more vigorous and it is easier to propagate. A lovely show plant that requires very little training.

Isle of Mull
Tolley, UK, 1978
Single. The tube is rose-pink veined in deeper rose. The sepals are a very pale pink with heavy rose veining at the base. The corolla is a striking rose-magenta, very deep in colour at the edges of the petals but paler at the base. The flower shape is unusual, reminiscent of a pagoda, and the blooms are very freely produced. The foliage is pale green and the growth upright, very bushy, and compact. 'Isle of Mull' makes a neat show plant but does not seem to be as popular as it deserves to be.

Jack Shahan
Tiret, USA, 1948
Single. The tube and sepals are deep pink and the corolla is very similar in colour. The flowers are quite large and freely produced. The young leaves are mid-green, maturing to a bronzed green. Cuttings of 'Jack Shahan' tend to root slowly and spasmodically but very few are actually lost. The growth is vigorous but lax, and this is an excellent cultivar for a hanging basket or weeping standard. It is often confused with 'Jack Acland' produced by Haag & Son in the United States (1952), but, although the flowers are almost identical, the growth of 'Jack Acland' is a little more upright.

Joan Pacey
Gadsby, UK, 1972
Single. The long tube is white flushed with pink and the sepals are pale pink. The long corolla is a similar shade of pink with deep pink veining. The growth is upright and very bushy and the foliage light green. The medium-sized flowers are exceptionally freely produced from early to late in the season. A reliable plant, easily trained for show work, whose only fault is its susceptibility to attack by red spider mites.

La Campanella
Blackwell, UK, 1968
Single or semi-double. The fairly small flowers are very freely produced. The short tube and sepals are white with a slight

tinge of pink and the corolla is a beautiful shade of bright blue-purple that fades to deep lavender with age. The foliage is small and dark green. The growth is short jointed, self-branching, and forms a wiry bush. This cultivar makes a beautiful hanging basket; it is possible to achieve with it a complete ball of flowers.

Lakeside
Thornley, UK, 1967
Single. The tube and sepals are pink-red and the sepals have green tips. The corolla is blue-violet veined with pink fading to lilac in the mature flowers. The foliage is dark green and the extremely vigorous growth is trailing in habit. A very free-flowering cultivar from early in the season until late autumn. The plant is self cleaning, dropping the fruits formed as well as the old flowers. An established favourite in hanging-basket classes at shows, it will also make a delightful standard.

Lena
Bunney, UK, 1862
Semi-double. The short fat tube is pale pink and the broad sepals are a slightly deeper shade of pink fading towards the tube. The corolla is a deep rose-magenta with a pale pink flush at the base of the petals. An early-flowering cultivar and extremely floriferous. The foliage is dark green and shiny. The growth is vigorous, self-branching, and lax. 'Lena' has proved reliably hardy in cultivation. Its rather prostrate habit is a disadvantage in the garden because the blooms tend to trail on the soil. It is, however, one of the best cultivars ever introduced for show work and makes an excellent basket or standard. A sport from it, 'Golden Lena', is a most attractive variegated form and is as hardy as its parent although less vigorous. 'Lena' appears to be identical with 'Eva Boerg', introduced by Yorke in Britain (1943).

Leonora
Tiret, USA, 1960
Single. The tube and sepals are a soft pink and the sepals that eventually recurve to touch the tube are tipped with green. The bell-shaped corolla is the same soft pink, lightly veined with a deeper pink and paler at the base of the petals. 'Leonora' is an early-flowering cultivar with medium-sized blooms that will make a lovely bush, standard, or pillar. It shows good weather resistance, and is an ideal patio-tub subject. The growth is upright, bushy, and vigorous. The foliage is mid-green. A plant that is easy to grow and propagates well. Awarded the American Fuchsia Society's Certificate of Merit (1964).

Loni Jane
Wood, USA, 1985
Double. The long tube is pale pink and the sepals, which recurve at the tips, are white, shading to pink at the base. The very full, flared corolla is white veined with pink. The leaves are large and mid-green. The growth is trailing and self-branching and suitable for growing in a hanging basket. This is a large flowered seedling from 'White King' and 'Pink Marshmallow' (see page 134).

Lord Lonsdale
Raiser unknown, UK, date unknown
Single. A medium-to-large flower in an outstanding colour combination. The tube and sepals are a pale tangerine orange and the corolla a much deeper shade of the same orange. The growth is bushy but somewhat lax and the mid-green foliage is heavily serrated and curled. The curling of the leaves is much more pronounced during the winter months when the plants are not in active growth and also when the cuttings are just rooted. This cultivar is similar to 'Aurora Superba', whose leaves are even more contorted. 'Lord Lonsdale' is not difficult to grow but it requires a lot of attention to cultivate a well-shaped plant.

Malibu Mist
Stubbs, USA, 1985
Double. The short tube and sepals are white but become pink with age. The sepals are tinged with pink on their underside and the tips recurve. The corolla opens

blue-violet splashed with pink and matures to a mauve-purple with a white centre. The contrast between the new and old blooms is most striking. The large full blooms are carried on stiff, trailing growth that can be trained as a lax bush or grown in a hanging basket.

Mantilla
Reiter, USA, 1948
A Triphylla-type single flower. The entire flower is a deep carmine with an exceptionally long tube, up to $3\frac{1}{2}$in (9cm). The small petals are spreading and the sepals pagoda-like. The habit is cascading with willowy, branching growth. The leaves are bronzed and a superb foil for the rich colour of the flowers. Young plants are susceptible to botrytis. 'Mantilla' requires a higher temperature than most to do well. It will make a very beautiful hanging basket. It was the first cultivar to be registered (as A.F.S 1) under the system introduced by the American Fuchsia Society in 1948.

Marcus Graham
Stubbs, USA, 1985
Double. The long tube is white flushed with beige-pink. The sepals, fully reflexed, twisting and curling against the tube are beige-pink with a tinge of dusky pink. The large, flared corolla is a dusky pink streaked with pale orange. The very large blooms are quite freely produced on upright growth. The leaves are mid-green and serrated at the edge. This cultivar is easily trained for the showbench.

Marinka
Rozain-Boucharlat, France, 1902
Single. The tube and sepals are a deep red and the corolla just a slightly deeper shade of the same colour. Produced in abundance, the flowers are medium in size and sometimes give the appearance of being semi-double. The foliage is dark green with red veining and with the dark red flowers can give the plant a rather sombre look unless it is grown in a bright position. It is probably the most popular trailer ever introduced. 'Marinka' makes an excellent

show plant and is a lovely subject for weeping standards and pillars as well as for growing as an espalier.

Mayblossom
Pacey, UK, 1984
Double. Small, very full double flowers are produced in profusion. The tube and sepals are rose pink and the corolla white flushed with rose. The growth is naturally trailing but compact and short jointed and the foliage is small. The overall petiteness of this cultivar makes it a good subject for a table standard, but 'Mayblossom' is equally suitable for basket work.

Mieke Meursing
Hopwood, UK, 1968
Single to semi-double. Originally described as a single but after twenty years in cultivation is found more often to be semi-double. The tube and sepals are red and the corolla pink with red veining. The mass of bloom is produced on upright, bushy, and compact growth. The grey-green foliage unfortunately gives the plant a rather dull appearance, which probably accounts for its lack of popularity. The enthusiasm of exhibitors for this cultivar more than compensates for its lack of general appeal and it is regularly seen as a prizewinner on the showbench. It received the British Fuchsia Society's Award of Merit (1968) and was chosen by the Netherlands Fuchsia Society to be named after their first President, Mrs Mieke Meursing, in 1969 on her retirement.

Minirose
de Graaf, Netherlands, 1983
Single. The tube is beige and the sepals are beige flushed with rose. The recurving sepal tips are dark rose. The sepals only just reveal the dark rose-coloured corolla that fades with maturity. The flowers are very small, borne in profusion, semi-erect, and long lasting. The growth is compact, upright, and bushy and the leaves are small. It is ideal as a small bush or table standard and is increasingly seen as a prizewinner on the showbench. A delightful novelty.

Mission Bells
Walker and Jones, USA, 1948
Single, occasionally semi-double. The tube and sepals are scarlet and the corolla a rich purple with red splashes towards the base of the petals. The bell-shaped flowers are freely produced on strong, upright growth. An extremely vigorous cultivar that is often offered by nurseries as a hardy but is not reliably so and, even if it survives, it flowers rather late in the season. It makes a lovely bush and is a good fuchsia for planting out for the summer in the garden or in patio tubs.

Moonlight Sonata
Blackwell, UK, 1963
Single. The tube and sepals are bright pink and the long sepals recurve until they almost touch the tube, revealing the light purple corolla and long style. The petals are flushed and veined with pink at the base. The medium-sized flowers are very freely produced on trailing growth. The foliage is mid-green and the leaves are serrated at the edges. A good cultivar for a hanging basket and one that also makes an attractive weeping standard.

Morning Light
Waltz, USA, 1960
Double. The tube is pink and the broad sepals are white, flushed lightly with pink. The very full corolla is a beautiful lavender-blue splashed with pink at the base of the petals. Altogether this is a well-formed large flower in a delightful colour combination. The foliage is yellow-green and the growth upright, bushy, and self-branching. 'Morning Light' grows well in the summer and roots easily but is rather susceptible to botrytis in the winter months.

Mrs Popple
Elliot, UK, 1899
Single. A medium-sized flower with a very short bulbous tube and non-recurving, bright scarlet sepals. The corolla is deep violet-purple that fades to a red-purple. The petals are flushed and veined with red at the base. The dark green, shiny leaves are produced on very strong, upright growth that arches gracefully when the plant comes into flower. 'Mrs Popple' was awarded a First Class Certificate by Britain's Royal Horticultural Society in its 1963–5 trials at Wisley. It is reliably hardy. One of the first garden fuchsias to come into flower, it quite often has a few flowers left into December. This is a superb garden plant and an ideal subject for a fuchsia hedge.

Northumbrian Belle
Ryle-Atkinson, UK, 1973
Single. The short tube and long, narrow sepals are rose pink. The sepals recurve until they almost touch the tube. The corolla is deep blue and the petals are flushed and streaked at the base with rose pink. The medium-to-large flowers are carried on strong, upright growth that is naturally self-branching and requires very little support even when the plant is in flower. The foliage is dark green, but this cultivar has a high nitrogen requirement and the leaves become bronzed if the plant is underfed. A free-flowering cultivar suitable for bush, standard, or pyramid.

Orange Crush
Handley, UK, 1972
Single. The tube and sepals are pale salmon-orange and the corolla deep orange. The blooms are medium in size and the sepals do not recurve. The flowers are very freely produced on an extremely upright, vigorous bush. The foliage is mid-green and the leaves serrated at the edges. A strong-growing cultivar, suitable for summer bedding or patio tubs.

Orange Mirage
Tiret, USA, 1970
Single. The tube and sepals are a deep salmon. The sepals, which recurve for half their length, are tipped with green. The rather long corolla is a deep, dull orange. The dark green leaves are borne on vigorous, horizontal growth that cascades when the plant is in bloom. A trouble-free cul-

tivar suitable for a large hanging basket, or as a standard or pillar, but one that, because of its vigour, requires more training than most to form a well-shaped plant.

Our Ted
Goulding, UK, 1987
Single. A new addition to the Triphylla-type cultivars, welcome because its flowers are white with just a suggestion of pink. The long, tapering tube and sepals are white with just a hint of pink at the tips. The corolla is white with a slight pink flush and opens a little wider than that of most of the Triphylla-type cultivars. The blooms are very freely produced on the ends of sturdy, upright stems. The foliage is very dark green and a perfect foil for the lovely flowers. It was named after a British grower, Ted Stiff of the East Anglian Society, who is well known for his prize-winning fuchsias.

Pee Wee Rose
Niederholzer, USA, 1939
Single or semi-double. The tube is pink-red and the sepals, which do not recurve or even open flat, are rose-red. The corolla is a mauvish-red when the flower first opens but fades to a similar red to the sepals. The flowers are small and very freely produced. When planted in the garden the growth is vigorous and upright, but it is more lax and willowy under glass. The leaves are very small. In Britain it received an Award of Merit from the Royal Horticultural Society in hardy trials at Wisley (1975–8).

Pink Galore
Walker, USA, 1958
Double. The long tube and reflexing sepals are a slightly deeper shade of candy pink than the well-formed corolla. One of the best true pink double-flowered fuchsias available, although it needs to be grown in the shade or the flower colour will deepen. The foliage is dark, shiny green and appears almost bronzed on a mature plant. The willowy trailing growth is most effective in a hanging basket, but this is not a terribly vigorous cultivar and more plants

than usual will be required to produce a good one. Unfortunately the flowers are produced on the ends of the trailing growth, leaving the top of the basket rather bare. Awarded the American Fuchsia Society's Certificate of Merit (1961).

Pink Marshmallow
Stubbs, USA, 1971
Double. The tube is pale pink and the broad sepals are white with a very slight pink overlay, especially where they join the tube. The very full corolla is white with just a hint of pink veining. The inner petals elongate, giving the blooms a double-skirted effect. When grown in full sunlight the pink overlay and veining become much more pronounced. The blooms are freely produced, which is unusual with very-large-flowered fuchsias. The foliage is a pale yellow-green and the habit trailing but bushy. A vigorous cultivar that makes an excellent large basket.

Plenty
Gadsby, UK, 1974
Single. The thick tube and sepals are red. The corolla is violet-purple flushed and streaked at the base of the petals with red. The flowers are, as the name suggests, produced in profusion and held almost upright. It is a seedling from 'Lady Isobel Barnett' (see page 91) and even more free flowering than its parent. The growth is upright, bushy, and short-jointed and the rather large leaves are dark green. An excellent cultivar for show work, making a superb bush even in a small pot. It is also hardy in many areas of Britain.

Prelude
Kennett, USA, 1958
Double. The tube is deep pink and the fully reflexed sepals white flushed with pink. The corolla is multi-coloured in royal purple, pink, and white. When the large flower first opens the outer, small, white petals are visible, but these open up to reveal the deep royal purple and pink splashed petals within. The growth is trailing and the long stems need to be

pinched frequently to train this cultivar into a reasonable hanging basket. There is another fuchsia available under the name 'Prelude' – a medium-sized, red/magenta, single-flowered, hardy cultivar raised by Blackwell in Britain (1957).

Preston Guild
Thornley, UK, 1971
Single. A small flower with white tube and sepals that completely recurve but do not hide the tube. The corolla is a glowing, deep blue that fades to mauve with age. The flowers are freely produced on vigorous, upright, but initially rather slender stems. The small foliage is mid-green. An excellent bush cultivar, suitable for bedding in the garden or in patio tubs. When grown in full sun the colour of the flower becomes flushed with pink and is not so attractive. 'Preston Guild' is hardy in a sheltered position in most areas in Britain.

Rading's Karin
Reimann, Netherlands, c.1983
A species hybrid of the Encliandra type with tiny flowers and foliage. The tube and sepals are deep rose-pink and the corolla is suffused with orange. The growth is spreading and semi-prostrate. This cultivar is hardy in a sheltered position in the garden.

Raspberry
Tiret, USA, 1959
Double. The tube and long sepals are white flushed with pink. The sepals that recurve to hide the tube are tipped with green. The very full corolla is a beautiful shade of raspberry pink, hence the name. The growth is upright and bushy and the foliage is dark green. Not an early flowering cultivar but useful for autumn show work, when many cultivars are past their best.

Red Ace
Roe, UK, 1983
Double. The short tube and reflexing sepals are scarlet. The corolla is a dusky red. The medium-sized flowers are freely produced on growth that is vigorous and upright, requiring very little support. The stems are red and the leaves dark green. Under glass 'Red Ace' will make a very large specimen plant, either as a bush, pillar, or standard, and it has also shown promise as a hardy garden plant in recent trials.

Ronald L. Lockerbie
Richardson, Australia, 1986
Double. The tube is carmine striped with light green. The long, broad sepals with twisted, recurved tips are creamy white flushed with carmine. The large, flared corolla opens creamy white and fades with age to white. This cultivar has been sold as the first yellow fuchsia because it reputedly throws an occasional yellow flower that fades to cream with age. During the past year, its performance in Britain has been disappointing, none of the flowers being anything other than cream, but this may be due to our different climate and soil conditions. The mid-green leaves are borne on arching, lax growth and this cultivar is suitable for a hanging basket. It is registered as cold hardy to 21°F (-6°C).

Rose of Castile
Banks, UK, 1855
Single. The tube and sepals are white and the corolla a light blue-purple. The petals are flushed with white at the base. The medium-sized flowers are very freely produced on strong, upright growth. 'Rose of Castile' is reliably hardy in cultivation. Under glass it makes a fine show plant; it is particularly good as a standard.

Rose Phenomenal
Raiser unknown
Double. The short tube and broad, reflexing sepals are scarlet and the full corolla a strong lavender pink. The flowers are large, well formed, and freely produced. The growth is strong and upright and very sturdy; the leaves are dark green. This is probably a sport from 'Phenomenal' raised by Lemoine in France (1869). Both these cultivars are now difficult to obtain; most nurseries offering 'Phenomenal' actually

supply the similarly flowered 'Royal Velvet' (see page 52). 'Rose Phenomenal' is an excellent garden plant that has shown promise of hardiness in recent trials.

Rosy Frills
Handley, UK, 1979
Double. The tube is greenish white and the short, broad sepals are very pale pink on the upper surface and a deeper shade underneath. The corolla is rose-pink edged with red and the outer petals are streaked with salmon. The large blooms are unusually abundant and produced from early in the season. The dark green foliage is borne on lax, trailing growth and the stems are red. A good show plant that can be grown as a lax bush, basket, or weeping standard.

Rubens
Meteor, Europe, c.1880
Single. The tube and sepals are a shiny scarlet-red and the corolla is deep purple. The foliage is yellow-green when young but matures to a delightful burnished copper that is particularly pronounced when the plant is grown in full light. The growth is strong but lax and 'Rubens' can be used in large hanging baskets to great effect. The medium-sized flowers are produced rather late in the season but the colour of the leaves is so remarkable that this cultivar can be grown for its foliage alone. 'Rubens' is also known as 'Burning Bush' and in Britain is listed by most nurseries as 'Autumnale'.

Rufus
Nelson, USA, 1952
Single. The tube, sepals, and corolla are all bright red. The medium-sized flowers are produced on very strong upright growth. This cultivar blooms over a long season and is a reliable large exhibition plant. Very large standards, pillars, or cordons can be easily grown as the plant is extremely robust and free from pest and disease. A lovely bright garden plant that has proved reliably hardy. Frequently referred to and catalogued, incorrectly, as 'Rufus the Red'.

Santa Cruz
Tiret, USA, 1947
A semi-double that has the appearance of a double. The bright red tube and sepals recurve to touch the tube. The corolla is a dusky purple-red that hardly fades with maturity. The flowers are fairly freely produced on strong, upright, bushy growth that arches gracefully when in bloom. The leaves are dark green with red veining. A good cultivar for flower arranging that stands well in water. It is hardy in most areas of Britain.

Shy Lady
Waltz, USA, 1955
Double. The short tube and broad, pointed sepals that recurve at the tips are white. The corolla of the newly opened flower is a creamy white that matures to a very pale peach. The medium-sized flowers are freely produced and the dainty, pastel blooms show to advantage against the dark green foliage. The habit is bushy and upright and suitable for the showbench.

Silver Anniversary
Stubbs, USA, 1985
Double. The tube and reflexing sepals are white and the underside of the sepals is flushed with orchid-pink. The corolla opens a pale silvery blue and matures to a deeper shade. The medium-to-large blooms are quite freely produced. The foliage is mid green and carried on stiff, trailing growth. A good cultivar for a hanging basket, but with support it can be trained as an upright bush.

Smokey Mountain
Wood, USA, 1987
Double. The wide tube is deep pink and the reflexing sepals are white, flushed with pink on the upper surface, pink on the underside, and green tipped. The corolla is a dusky purple maturing to dusky mauve. The flower colour is at its best when the plant is grown in the shade. The foliage is dark green and carried on trailing, self-branching growth. A beautiful cultivar for a hanging basket or weeping standard.

Southgate

Walker and Jones, USA, 1951

Double. The tube and sepals, which are held out from the corolla but do not recurve, are pink. The corolla is a paler shade of the same pink and the petals are lightly veined in the deeper pink. The growth is sturdy, bushy, and upright. The foliage is very deep green and the stems are red. This is one of the best American cultivars and it can be trained into any form, including a hanging basket. It is an easy cultivar for the beginner and highly recommended for a first attempt at growing a standard.

Stanley Cash

Pennisi, USA, 1970

Double. The large, fat buds are white; the tube and sepals open a waxy white and the sepals recurve just at the tips. The very full corolla is deep blue-purple. The large blooms are freely produced from early in the season. The foliage is dark green and serrated at the edge. The stems are pale greeny-white. The growth is vigorous and lax. This cultivar will make a lovely hanging basket or standard and with support can be trained into a good bush. One of the best plants in this colour range and size of flower.

Swingtime

Tiret, USA, 1950

Double. The tube and sepals are bright, shiny red and the sepals are held back from the corolla. The full, double corolla is creamy white and the bases of the petals are veined in red. The growth is initially upright but trails under the weight of the large blooms. The foliage is mid-green and a perfect foil for the striking colour combination of the flowers. A superb fuchsia that makes a beautiful basket, standard, or espalier, 'Swingtime' is remarkably weather resistant and can be used as a summer bedding plant in the garden or in patio tubs. There is also available a sport with golden foliage, 'Golden Swingtime', which occurred in several nurseries in the same year (1981).

Texas Longhorn

Walker, USA, 1960

Semi-double or double. The tube and very long sepals are red and the corolla white but veined with red. It is the length of the horizontally held sepals that gives this fuchsia a reputation for having very large flowers, because the corolla is relatively small. The growth is willowy and trailing. A difficult cultivar to grow well, 'Texas Longhorn' is probably at its best planted in a hanging basket, although with patience it can be trained into a reasonable standard. An over-rated fuchsia that will probably decline in popularity as the very large double-flowered cultivars such as 'Garden Week' from Australia and New Zealand become more widely grown.

Ting-a-Ling

Schnabel, USA, 1959

Single. An all-white flower with only a faint pink blush on the tube that becomes more pronounced in full light. The long, pointed sepals recurve to reveal the bell-shaped corolla. An extremely free-flowering cultivar. The growth is upright and bushy and the foliage mid-green. Like most white-flowered cultivars it is susceptible to botrytis and can be difficult to root and grow. However, with perseverance, it can be trained into a beautiful standard.

Tom Thumb

Baudinat, France, 1850

Single. Tiny flowers freely produced. The tube and sepals are red and the corolla purple. The growth is upright, very bushy, and dwarf. This cultivar has given rise to two sports, 'Lady Thumb' (red and white) and 'Son of Thumb' (red and lavender). All three 'Thumbs' are reliably hardy. The dwarf growth makes them ideal subjects for a small-pot class on the showbench. They may also be grown as rockery plants or at the front of a shrub border.

Trail Blazer

Reiter, USA, 1951

Double. The tube and sepals are pale dusky red and the corolla a much deeper shade of dusky red. The growth is vigorous and cascading and the quite large flowers are borne on the ends of the trailing stems. This cultivar is an excellent choice for a large hanging basket or it makes a lovely weeping standard.

Trumpeter
Reiter, USA, 1946

Single of the Triphylla type with characteristically long flowers produced in clusters at the end of the stems. The long tube and sepals are a deep salmon pink and the corolla a slightly deeper shade of the same colour. The short, pointed sepals are held just away from the corolla. An extremely free-flowering cultivar. The growth is cascading, short jointed, and compact. The dark, bluish green foliage becomes bronzed with maturity and is a most attractive foil for the deep pink flowers. A rather slow-growing cultivar that is suitable for a small hanging basket.

Westminster Chimes
Clyne, UK, 1976

Semi-double. The tube and sepals are deep pink and the sepals are held horizontally. The corolla is violet-blue, flushed with pink at the base of the petals. This is a very compact cultivar with correspondingly small leaves and flowers. The habit is initially upright and willowy, but the stems trail under the weight of blooms produced. An excellent show plant that can be relied on to cover itself in flowers. This cultivar can be trained as a bush, small standard, or for a hanging basket.

White Pixie
Merrist Wood, UK, 1968

Single. The short tube and recurving sepals are bright red and the corolla creamy white with red veining. The foliage is yellow with pronounced red veining and the stems are also red. The vigorous growth is bushy, upright, and arching. This is a sport of 'Pixie', itself a sport of 'Graf Witte'. The foliage of 'White Pixie' is yellower than that of its parents. Hardy

White Spider
Haag, USA, 1951

Single. The tube and sepals are a very pale pink. The sepals reflex and twist away from the corolla, which is white tinged with palest pink. The medium-sized flowers are freely produced from early in the season but, despite the white in its name, the blooms are always noticeably flushed with pink. The growth is strong and horizontal.

Winston Churchill
Garson, USA, 1942

Double. The long tube and broad sepals are red. The green-tipped sepals reflex to hide the tube. The corolla is a deep lavender blue flushed and streaked with pink at the base of the petals. The medium-to-large blooms are very freely produced on strong, upright, bushy, short-jointed growth. The foliage is dark green and the leaves rather long and pointed. An extremely sturdy grower that requires little support and very little training. One of the most reliable plants for the showbench, as a bush, standard, pillar, or pyramid.

RECOMMENDED CULTIVARS

To train as bushes

Annabel
Beacon Rosa
Belsay Beauty
Bishop's Bells
Blue Elf
Bon Accorde
Bountiful
Caroline
Celia Smedley
Checkerboard
Cliff's Unique
Cloverdale Jewel
Cloverdale Pearl
Collingwood
Coquet Bell
Coquet Dale
Cotton Candy
Countess of Aberdeen
Curly Q
Dancing Flame
Dark Eyes
Display
Dollar Princess
Flirtation Waltz
Gartenmeister Bonstedt
Gilda
Hampshire Beauty
Hampshire Blue
Hampshire Treasure
Heidi Ann
Iced Champagne
Joan Pacey
Lady Isobel Barnett
Lady Kathleen Spence
Leonora
Linda Goulding

Loeky
Marin Glow
Mieke Meursing
Miss California
Mission Bells
Morning Light
Nancy Lou
Nellie Nuttall
Northumbrian Belle
Orange Drops
Our Ted
Pacquesa
Peppermint Stick
Plenty
R.A.F.
Red Ace
Rose of Castile
Royal Velvet
Ruth King
Snowcap
Snowfire
Southgate
Spion Kop
String of Pearls
Tennessee Waltz
Ting-a-Ling
Tom Thumb (and sports)
Traudchen Bonstedt
White Pixie
Winston Churchill

To train as standards

Annabel
Barbara
Beacon Rosa
Bicentennial
Blue Elf

Bountiful
Checkerboard
Cliff's Unique
Cloverdale Jewel
Cloverdale Pearl
Constellation
Coquet Bell
Coquet Dale
Cotton Candy
Dancing Flame
Dark Eyes
Display
Garden News
Gilda
Golden Marinka
Hampshire Blue
Hampshire Treasure
Harry Gray
Heidi Ann
Iced Champagne
Jeane
Joan Pacey
Lady Kathleen Spence
Leonora
Loeky
Marin Glow
Marinka
Nancy Lou
Peppermint Stick
Phyllis
R.A.F.
Rose of Castile
Rose of Denmark
Royal Velvet
Rufus
Snowcap
Southgate
Spion Kop

Swingtime
Tennessee Waltz
White Pixie
Winston Churchill

For hanging baskets

Applause
Auntie Jinks
Autumnale
Baby Pink
Bicentennial
Bouffant
Brookwood Joy
Cascade
Celadore
City of Adelaide
Crackerjack
Derby Imp
Doreen Stroud
Gay Fandango
Gilda
Golden Marinka
Hampshire Treasure
Harry Gray
Hula Girl
Jack Shahan
Kegworth Carnival
La Campanella

Lakeside
Lena
Mantilla
Marinka
Mayblossom
Molesworth
Moonlight Sonata
Pink Galore
Pink Marshmallow
Rose of Denmark
Rough Silk
Sophisticated Lady
Southgate
Stanley Cash
Swingtime
Trail Blazer
Trumpeter

For hardiness

Abbé Farges
Alice Hoffman
Army Nurse
Beacon
Blue Bush
Brutus
C. J. Howlett
Charming
Chillerton Beauty

Cliff's Hardy
Clifton Charm
Dollar Princess
Empress of Prussia
Florence Turner
Frau Hilde Rademacher
*F. magellanica v.
    macrostemma
    'Versicolor'*
F. procumbens
Garden News
Hawkshead
Heidi Ann
Jeane
Lady Thumb
Margaret
Margaret Brown
Monsieur Thibaut
Mr A. Huggett
Mrs Popple
Prosperity
Rose of Castile Improved
Rufus
Santa Cruz
Sharpitor
Tennessee Waltz
Tom Thumb
Trase
White Pixie

SOCIETIES

Australia
Australian Fuchsia Society
Box No.97
P.O. Norwood
South Australia 5067

Denmark
Dansk Fuchsia Club
Secretariat
V/Merete Printz
Frugtparken 1
2820 Gentofte

New Zealand
New Zealand Fuchsia Society
c/o P.O. Box 11–082
Ellerslie
Auckland 5

United Kingdom
The British Fuchsia Society
29, Princes Crescent
Dollar
Central
Scotland

United States of America
The American Fuchsia Society
County Fair Building
9th Avenue and Lincoln Way
San Francisco
California 94122

GARDENS TO VISIT

United Kingdom

Akenfield, Charlsfield, Suffolk
Clapton Court Gardens, Crewkerne, Somerset
Harlow Car Gardens, Crag Lane, Harrogate, North Yorkshire
Longleat House, Longleat, Wiltshire
Powis Castle, Welshpool, Powys
Wallington House, Cambo, Northumberland
Wisley Gardens (R.H.S.), Wisley, Surrey

United States

Descanso Gardens, La Canada, California
Fuchsia Land, Centinela Avenue, Los Angeles, California
Lakeside Park Gardens, Bellevue Avenue, Oakland, California
Rosecroft Begonia Gardens, Silvergate Avenue, Point Loma, San Diego, California

BIBLIOGRAPHY

Checklist of Fuchsias Registered, American Fuchsia Society Staff, ed., Eureka, California: American Fuchsia Society, 1973–1983.

Fuchsia Culture, American Fuchsia Society Staff, ed., Eureka, California: American Fuchsia Society, 1984.

Fuchsia Judging School Manual & AFS Judging Rules, American Fuchsia Society Staff, ed., Eureka, California: American Fuchsia Society, 1986.

The New A to Z on Fuchsias, Bill Barnes, Long Beach, California: National Fuchsia Society, 1976.

The Checklist of Species, Hybrids and Cultivars of the Genus Fuchsia, L.B. Boullemier, Poole: Blandford Press, 1985.

Fuchsias for House and Garden, Sidney Clapham, Newton Abbot: David & Charles, 1982 and New York: Universe Publishing Co., 1982.

Fuchsias, Kew Gardening Guides, D.W.H. Clark, London: The Hamlyn Publishing Group, 1987.

The Oakleigh Guide to Fuchsias, D.W.H. Clark, Alresford: Oakleigh Publications, (revised edition) 1987.

Fuchsia Lexicon, R. Ewart, Poole: Blandford Press, 1982.

Growing Fuchsias, K. Jennings and V. Miller, Portland, Oregon: Timber Press, 1982.

Growing Fuchsias, Deborah Law, Erie, Pennsylvania: Kangaroo Court Publishing, 1985.

Fuchsias in Colour, B. and V. Proudley, Poole: Blandford Press, 1975.

A Colour Guide to Fuchsias, G. and A. Walker, Aughton: Grange Publications 1986.

A Second Colour Guide to Fuchsias, G. and A. Walker, Aughton: Grange Publications, 1986.

Fuchsias: A Wisley Handbook, G. Wells, London: Cassell/The Royal Horticultural Society, 1985.

Fuchsias, S.J. Wilson, London: Faber & Faber (revised edition) 1974.

GLOSSARY

Anther The tip of the stamen that bears the pollen.

Berry The fruit with the seeds embedded in the pulp.

Calyx That part of the flower made up of the sepals and tube.

Corolla That part of the flower made up of the petals.

Cultivar A plant that has been bred or particularly selected by man.

Filament The part of the stamen that supports the anther.

Frost protection Maintaining a temperature above freezing point.

Half-hardy Describes plants that may be bedded out during the summer months but need frost protection in the winter.

Hardy Describes plants that can be permanently planted in the garden (applied to fuchsias growing in countries where they are subjected to frost).

Hybrid A plant that is the result of a cross fertilization between two species.

Internode The length of stem between two leaf axils.

Leaf axil The point at which the leaf joins the stem and from which the side shoots are produced.

Leaf node The slightly swollen area from which the leaves grow.

Ovary The female part of the flower that contains the embryo seeds.

Petaloid In the fuchsia flower this refers to the small, short petals that occur at the base of the corolla. It also refers to parts of the flower, such as sepals and stamens, that assume petal-like structures.

Petiole The leaf stalk.

Pinching out (stopping) The removal of the growing tip of a stem.

Pistil The collective name for stigma, style, and ovary.

Pot back To remove the old compost from around the roots of a plant and replant with fresh compost in a smaller pot.

Pot on To remove a plant from a pot with minimal root disturbance and to place in a larger one with fresh compost.

Repot To remove a plant from its pot and shake off as much of the old compost as possible before replacing it, usually, in the same size pot with fresh compost.

Sepals The part of the flower apparent as the outside of the bud that opens out to reveal the corolla.

Species Recognizably distinct plants that occur in the wild and that breed true from seed.

Sport A flower or foliage variant of a cultivar or species.

Stamen The combined filament and anther.

Stigma The enlarged tip of the style that is receptive to pollen.

Style The connecting stalk between stigma and ovary.

Transpiration The loss of water mainly from the surface of the leaves and flowers.

Tube The elongated part of the calyx that joins the ovary to the sepals and corolla.

Variety A minor but distinct permanent variation of a species.

Woody growth Stems that have become thickened and brown with age, particularly at the base of the plant.

INDEX

Page numbers in **bold** refer to the captions to the colour plates.

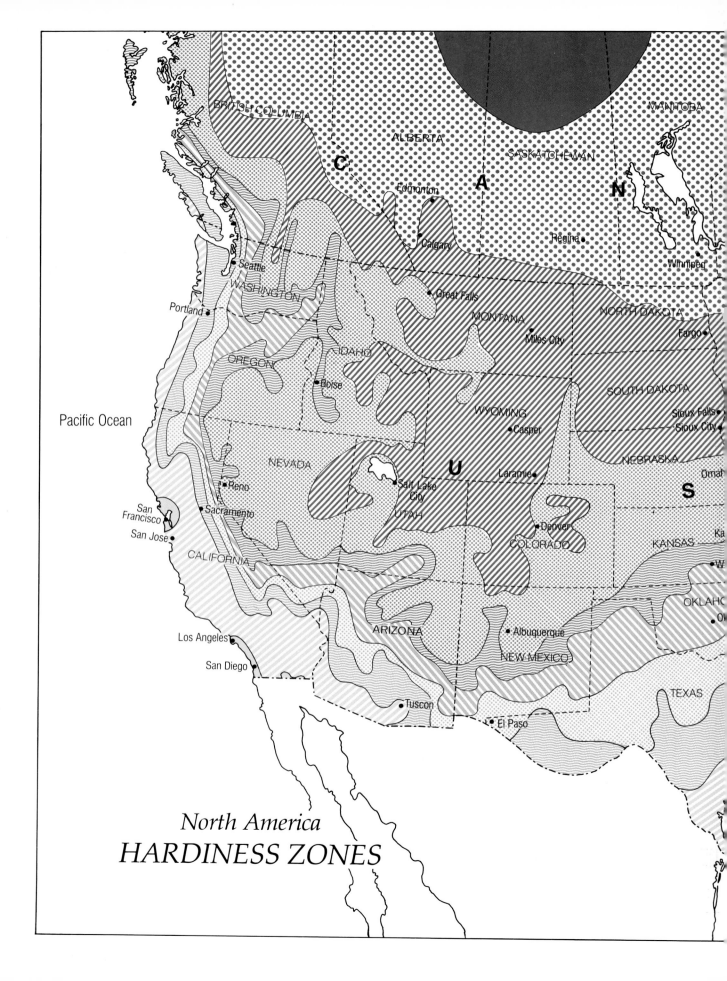

North America
HARDINESS ZONES